NIAGARA FALLS

in

WORLD WAR II

NIAGARA FALLS

in

WORLD WAR II

MICHELLE ANN KRATTS

THE
History
PRESS

Published by The History Press
Charleston, SC
www.historypress.net

First published 2016

Manufactured in the United States

ISBN 978.1.46713.737.9

Library of Congress Control Number: 2016943916

For my grandparents,
Thank you for your bravery, your indefatigable spirit and your stories of the
Greatest Generation.
PFC Arthur Emil Barthel, United States Army Air Forces and the
Electrometallurgical Company (Union Carbide)
Airman Henry Joseph Borgatti, Royal Canadian Air Force
Jean Fortuna Borgatti, Bell Aircraft Corporation and wartime bride
Johanna Knuppel Barthel, wartime bride

CONTENTS

ACKNOWLEDGEMENTS

When I was asked to write this book, my first feeling was of profound satisfaction. I realized at once that I have been preparing to write this book my entire life. Ever since I was a little girl, I have begged my grandparents to tell me stories about the war years. My work as a librarian at the Lewiston Public Library and as a historian for the city of Niagara Falls introduced me to an incredible number of war veterans and people who lived during that time. Through their stories, I learned to see the world through their eyes. I wasn't merely jotting down notes anymore; I was really there at the Battle of the Bulge, in the war factories, in the Philippines. I was there in Niagara Falls when those terrible black-rimmed letters came home. And then at victory…when all the church bells were chiming…I was there.

I also learned things about my own family. I had always wondered what happened to my grandfather Arthur Barthel. He suffered so acutely from a nervous condition following his service. Now I am wondering if his work in Niagara Falls' wartime factories and his exposure to hazardous materials before and during his time in the army (he served with a chemical company) may have contributed to his ill health and mental disposition. My research has proven that the homefront in cities like Niagara Falls may have been just as hazardous as the war zones.

I am so incredibly grateful to everyone who assisted me. Thank you to all the people who allowed me to interview them and to those who helped along the way: my inspiration, my wonderful grandmother Jean Borgatti;

my fabulous mother, Beverly Barthel, for scanning photos at a moment's notice; my dear friends Marcia Buzzelli and Maureen Weber; the Spacones; my neighbor Dominic Niccola; the O'Connors; the Paonessas; my good friend, the sweetest man in the world, Peter Vendrillo, who is always overflowing with stories of times past; Harold and Elaine Woodcock, who came from afar and shared information about their brother; Renee Peunic for arranging the meeting; and Lew Buttery for introducing me to his mother, Marie Myers, who had so many vivid memories of wartime Niagara Falls.

So many people graciously shared their photos, recipes and memories for this book. Thank you to my friends Pat DiNieri, Eleanor Novara, Susanne Shivery-Hake, Beverly Bidak, Peggy Taylor-Hulligan, Stephanie Golba, Jim Neiss, the Ventresca family, the Glasgow family, the Scime family, Jacob Henry, the Martinez family and Dan Lucarini.

Much gratitude to the Niagara Falls Public Library (Jennifer, Cecelia and Courtney) for putting up with my constant demands; to my director, Jill Palermo, and to my colleagues at the Lewiston Public Library, who found me a ghost of a staff member while writing this; to Jeff and Tereza at the Book Corner for getting the ball rolling; to Ray Meissner of the Aerospace Museum and Archives for assisting me with the history of Bell Aircraft, for scanning these wonderful photos and for proofreading the chapter on Bell Aircraft; to Hugh Neeson for sharing stories of wartime Bell Aircraft and also for proofreading the text; for Jason Parfinski from the Niagara Aerospace Museum for all his assistance; to my friend and colleague Gretchen Duling, PhD, for her assistance and insight concerning the wartime history of Fort Niagara; to author and historian Suzanne Simon Dietz for looking over various sections of the manuscript with the eyes of an expert; to the assistant director of the Old Fort Niagara Association, Jerome P. Brubaker, for jumping over hurdles in order to get these very important photos to me in time for the book, as well as for proofreading the text concerning Fort Niagara; to my DAR (Daughters of the American Revolution) sister Jan Johnpier for reading over and approving the story about the Victory cookbooks; to my friend and fellow librarian David Brooks for sharing his aunt's wartime scrapbook, statistical information and company newsletters from Niagara Falls–area plants and for proofreading the text; to my friend and colleague Pete Ames, town of Niagara historian, for his assistance with the Glasgow family and for proofreading the text; and to my friend and photographer Tim Baxter for taking some beautiful pictures for this book and also for graciously aiding me in all of my photo "situations."

Thank you to my friends and especially to my family for putting up with me through the process (in such haste!). So many days and nights I shamelessly rejected them for this book.

And special thanks to my brilliant editor, Karmen Q. Cook, for her special support and patience every step of the way and for bringing the idea of a book such as this to fruition.

INTRODUCTION

Since the very beginning, Niagara Falls has been a symbol of America's thunderous strength. Father Louis Hennepin, a missionary who accompanied the LaSalle expedition of 1678, was the first European to write at length of this wondrous cataract:

> *I wished a hundred times that somebody had been with us, who could have described the Wonders of this prodigious frightful fall, so as to give the Reader a just and natural Idea of it, such as might satisfy him, and create in him an Admiration of this Prodigy of Nature as great as it deserves.*[1]

Many others came after him and were driven to write of this powerful natural phenomenon as well. Author Nathaniel Hawthorne "threw" himself "on the earth," feeling that he was "unworthy to look at the Great Falls."[2] Artists came and set up camp, even during the icy winters, in hopes of capturing the essence of the waterfalls. Presidents came and stood fascinated at the brink. But perhaps President Abraham Lincoln summed it up most completely:

> *Niagara-Falls! By what mysterious power is it that millions and millions, are drawn from all parts of the world, to gaze upon Niagara Falls? It calls up the indefinite past. When Columbus first sought this continent—when Christ suffered on the cross—when Moses led Israel through the Red-Sea—nay, even, when Adam first came from the hand of his Maker—then as now, Niagara was roaring here.*[3]

At one time the city's slogan was "Power Unlimited, Beauty Unimpaired."[4] Niagara Falls was also commonly referred to as the Power City of the World.[5] The first recorded person to draw power from the water was Daniel Joncaire. In 1759, he dug a narrow ditch above the falls at Goat Island (a small island in the middle of Niagara Falls, located between the Bridal Veil Falls and the Horseshoe Falls) and used the water to turn a wheel in order to power a small sawmill. General Peter B. Porter and his brother, Augustus Porter, founding fathers of Niagara Falls, built an early water-powered gristmill and tannery near the site of Joncaire's mill. During the 1850s, the Niagara Falls Hydraulic Power and Manufacturing Company purchased water rights and began construction of a canal that would transport water from above the Falls to mill sites below the Falls. By 1881, the power company was able to deliver energy to electrify the city of Niagara Falls and power the mills. Jacob Schoellkopf, a German immigrant and successful businessman, purchased the hydraulic canal land and the water and power rights. He envisioned that the future of industry would involve the commercial production of electricity, and his company succeeded in establishing one of the first hydroelectric-generating stations in the world. Soon after, by the time Niagara Falls was officially incorporated as a city in 1892, all manner of industry flocked to the Power City of the World. Niagara Falls became an electrochemical center. Inevitably, the industry demanded thousands of laborers. At just about the same time, millions of immigrants were flooding in through our American borders in desperate need of work.

The immigrants mostly came from southern and eastern Europe. The author and historian Dr. H. William Feder wrote in his landmark work on the East Side community of Niagara Falls that "Niagara Falls became known for having the highest percentage of immigrants of any city in New York State outside of New York City."[6] Italian stonemasons expertly lined the tail-race tunnels with bricks. The Polish and Armenians worked alongside the Lebanese, the Lithuanians, the Spanish and the Croatians at the great furnaces of Niagara Falls' growing industrial complex. By 1940, African Americans, mostly from Alabama, were heading up north for work and a better way of life. Many had perceived Niagara Falls as "a better place to raise a family and prosper."[7] Companies such as the Aluminum Company of America (ALCOA), Carborundum, the Hooker Electrochemical Company, the Niagara Alkali Company, Kimberly-Clark, the Acheson Graphite Company, the Alox Corporation, the E.I. DuPont de Nemours Company, Mathieson Alkali Works, the National Carbon Company, Oldbury Electro Company, Niacet, the Ramapo Ajax Company and the Electrometallurgical

Company established themselves within the city during this time. By 1919, Niagara Falls was producing 35 percent of all chemicals in New York State and 5 percent of all electrical machinery.[8] Businesses grew out of demand. Tourists and honeymooners chose Niagara Falls as their favorite getaway. Niagara Falls had become an international destination. By 1930, when the Great Depression was in full swing, Niagara Falls had a population that swelled to over seventy thousand people, and much of the city was inhabited by immigrants and non-citizens. Cultures shifted dramatically. New ethnic traditions were finding their way into the fabric of Niagara's psyche. By 1940, the city of Niagara Falls had a population of close to eighty thousand people.[9]

On December 7, 1941, when Pearl Harbor was attacked, Niagara Falls found itself on a special stage set by nature and fate—a stage on which the bravest and finest were called to action. Our men and women, many from foreign lands, were ready to roll up their sleeves and take on the world. Those who left our shores to fight the enemy did so with courage and vitality. Those who stayed behind may have sacrificed a lot more than most people may realize. They kept the home fires burning and helped to ensure that the city of Niagara Falls, New York, would become a major player in a postwar world.

Chapter 1

IN A TOTAL WAR

THE FIRST TEN DAYS

It was a Sunday afternoon in Niagara Falls, New York, on December 7, 1941, when the Japanese launched their historic aerial attack against the United States Naval Base at Pearl Harbor in the territory of Hawaii. The weather was fair and cold. There were only fourteen shopping days until Christmas. The bustle of the holiday season was underway, but across the nation, the threat of war was unequivocal. There was a gathering storm. It could happen at any moment.

James W. MacKenzie spent the entire time of the attack watching *A Yank in the RAF*, starring Tyrone Power, at the Capitol Theatre on Niagara Street.[10] He and his sister arrived at the movies around 1:00 p.m. They were stunned by "the intense silence" they found upon arriving at their home later that afternoon. Their parents, immigrants from Britain, were glued to their Philco radio, awaiting updates on the situation. They had been worried for their family back home since 1939, but now they knew that "Britain no longer stood alone....the Yanks [were] coming."[11]

For those in Niagara Falls spending a tranquil afternoon before the radio, the announcement of the raid came through at about 2:30 p.m. *The World Today*, a radio news broadcast of the CBS Radio Network, first broke the story when John Daly reported, "We interrupt this program to bring you a special news bulletin. The Japanese have attacked Pearl Harbor, Hawaii, by air, President Roosevelt has just announced. The attack also was made on all naval and military activities on the principle [*sic*] island of Oahu."[12]

The USS *Arizona* was attacked at Pearl Harbor on December 7, 1941. *Courtesy National Parks Service.*

Almost immediately, Niagara Falls became an armed camp. As the protection of municipalities was considered of highest importance, a detachment of soldiers from Fort Niagara, a permanent army garrison located in nearby Youngstown, New York, arrived shortly after the attacks. They were to guard the power plants, bridges and other important locations against sabotage. Colonel Clayton J. Herman, acting commandant at Fort Niagara, holding this position due to the temporary absence of Colonel Floyd D. Carlock, was in charge of the guard detachment, along with a similar group assigned to Buffalo. Police forces, supplemented by volunteers of recently formed civil defense units, took elaborate steps to work alongside the military in an effort to maintain constant vigilance "at plants producing power, chemicals, airplanes and other war products, at points connecting with the Canadian border, on canals and public utilities, in railroad yards and at other vital stations."[13]

In addition to the precautionary measures taking place at the previously mentioned locations, army guards were stationed at the Bell Aircraft plant,

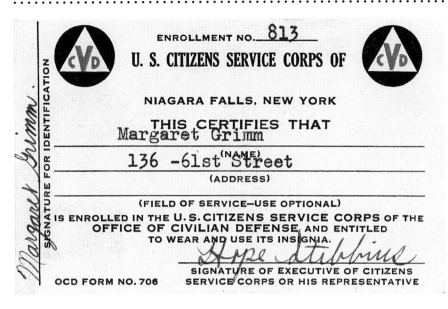

ENROLLMENT NO. 813

U. S. CITIZENS SERVICE CORPS OF

NIAGARA FALLS, NEW YORK

THIS CERTIFIES THAT

Margaret Grimm

(NAME)

136 -61st Street

(ADDRESS)

(FIELD OF SERVICE—USE OPTIONAL)

IS ENROLLED IN THE U. S. CITIZENS SERVICE CORPS OF THE OFFICE OF CIVILIAN DEFENSE, AND ENTITLED TO WEAR AND USE ITS INSIGNIA.

OCD FORM NO. 706

SIGNATURE OF EXECUTIVE OF CITIZENS SERVICE CORPS OR HIS REPRESENTATIVE

SIGNATURE FOR IDENTIFICATION

U.S. Citizens Service Corps card, Margaret Grimm. *Author's collection.*

located at the edge of Niagara Falls, in the town of Wheatfield, New York. Civilians were warned to stay away from the Niagara Falls Municipal Airport after sunset, and all private flying was suspended. The field was only to be used by army, navy and Bell test pilots and transport planes.

Niagara Falls mayor Ernest W. Mirrington Jr. read from a telegram from New York governor Herbert H. Lehman of instructions for civil defense authorities: "You are directed to take all steps necessary to prevent sabotage in defense plants, public utilities, water works, bridges and all other places of strategic importance in your jurisdiction and to protect all Japanese nationals residing in your city."[14]

Rob Roy MacLeod, chairman of the Niagara Falls Defense Council, immediately called for a special meeting of the council to consider emergency measures. Members of other civilian defense organizations such as the air raid wardens, auxiliary police and firemen's units stood ready for orders from the top.

Niagara Falls had actually been preparing for this fateful moment for quite some time. Almost two years before Pearl Harbor, the federal government had seen a need for an agency that could plan civil defense activities on a national scale and created the Office of Civil Defense (OCD). Fiorella LaGuardia was appointed director. The OCD was an independent agency and not associated with the United States Department of War.

Responsibilities for decisions and action remained with the local councils in each individual city and county.

Mayor Mirrington appointed the Niagara Falls Defense Council in February 1941. By the spring of 1941, Niagara Falls had participated in a statewide metal-working machinery survey to determine if idle machine tool capacity could be put to work on defense production. To the credit of the Niagara Falls Police Department, Niagara Falls was among the first cities to complete the task. Captain John Emerson conducted the council's aluminum scrap collection campaign, donating four tons of scrap at completion. The Niagara Falls Fire Department prepared it for shipment in a manner superior to other communities and elicited much praise. A housing survey was also completed by the Civilian Defense Council in order to identify any need for additional housing for new defense workers who might be called to the area as a result of a declaration of war.

After much planning, Niagara Falls was certainly prepared for whatever the future held. Perhaps most representative of the sudden changes to everyday life was the fact that the detective bureau of the Niagara Falls Police Department was turned over to the army. During the evening of December 7, 1941, Colonel Herman, who had arrived in Niagara Falls with his detachment from Fort Niagara, established headquarters there. "A sign was placed on the entrance door shortly before noon. It read: United States Army Headquarters."[15]

In Harm's Way

Although Niagara Falls, New York, was quite a distance from the area of conflict, there were men and women from Niagara Falls present at Pearl Harbor on December 7, 1941. They each lived through the ordeal and all the confusion that followed. Some did not survive the war. Some Niagara Falls survivors of the Japanese attack included the following: Seaman Second Class John L. Madera, United States Navy (501 Hyde Park Boulevard); Fireman First Class William Barr, United States Navy (573 Seventy-Eighth Street); Private First Class Samuel Ashker, United States Army Air Forces (1325½ Willow Avenue); Yeoman John H. Auchu, United States Navy (Seventy-Ninth Street); Private First Class James A. Rader, United States Army Air Forces (1118 Garden Avenue); Staff Sergeant Roy T. Pope, United States Army Air Forces (1848 Cleveland Avenue); Sergeant Anthony Pelsoni, United States

"Remember Pearl Harbor, Don't be caught with your pants down." *Courtesy Tim Baxter.*

Army Air Forces (2260 Ontario Avenue); Sergeant Joseph Golba, United States Army (2777 Monroe Avenue); Mrs. R.D. Blankenhorn (College Avenue); Mrs. Howard R. Fellenz (1653 Linwood Avenue); and Sergeant Thomas E. Ross, United States Army Air Forces (1315 Maple Avenue).

To the horror of the families, two of Niagara's witnesses at Pearl Harbor were initially incorrectly listed among the dead: Seaman Second Class John L. Madera and Fireman First Class William Barr. Shortly after the assault, on December 16, 1941, Mr. and Mrs. Fred Madera received the news in a telegram from Rear Admiral C.W. Nimitz, chief of the Bureau of Navigation of the Navy Department: "The Navy Department deeply regrets to inform you that your son, John Loughton Madera, Seaman Second Class, United States Navy, was lost in action in the performance of his duty and in the service of his country. The department extends to you its sincerest sympathy in your great loss."[16]

John was a young man, not yet twenty. He had been recently employed with the Civilian Conservation Corps (CCC) as a latrine orderly in Niagara

Falls. It was stated in the *Niagara Falls Gazette* that Seaman Madera had the distinct honor of being "the first Niagara Falls man officially reported killed in action in the war since the United States entered."[17] But another telegram arrived. Posted by airmail from the fleet post office, Pearl Harbor, it said the following: "Everything is ok with me. Please don't worry about anything. I will write a letter later when I get a chance."[18]

The letter was from John himself. Because of navy censorship, it was impossible to determine the time or date of the stamp. Local postal officials believed that the postcard would have required at least three days to be received in Niagara Falls from Pearl Harbor. In other words, it had to have been written after the invasion.

John's family was not new to the vagaries of war. His father, Frederick George Madera, was a hero of the First World War. He had served with the Canadian and American armies and had received numerous decorations, including a Purple Heart for wounds received in action. Following the war, he was very active in veterans' organizations. He was the organizer and the first president of Branch No. 51 of the Canadian Legion of the British Empire Service League. John's brother, Frederick, also served in the army during the Second World War.

Other cases of men killed in action were also erroneous. The navy's records were incomplete, and casualty reports were often wrong. As some of the enlisted men had neglected to report back to their officers during the attack, they were assumed dead—especially if they were known to have been on or near ships that were damaged or destroyed. If there was no record stating that they had reported to officers, it was assumed they were missing or dead. Following the complaints that naturally arose from this situation, the navy promised "more information within a few days."[19]

Finally, on New Year's night, the Madera family received yet another telegram that stated that John L. Madera, of Niagara Falls, was very much alive. "I was sure that he was still alive," Mrs. Madera said.[20] John Madera survived that fateful day in December 1941 and served faithfully throughout the war. He lived a long life and passed away in South Carolina on September 27, 1998.

The other Niagaran reported killed in action was Fireman First Class William Barr. He was the second man from Niagara Falls reported killed in the raid. Mrs. Alice Barr, William's mother, received a telegram, also signed by Rear Admiral C.W. Nimitz (who was named commander of the Pacific Fleet on December 17), that reported her son had been "lost in action in the performance of his duty and in the service of his country."[21]

Soon after, Mrs. Barr received a postcard, mailed December 9 by her son, bearing the simple message: "I am well."[22] Like the Madera family, Mrs. Barr eventually received another telegram from Washington, D.C., expressing regret for any anxiety caused by this situation.

Private First Class Samuel Ashker, the son of Lebanese immigrants Elias Joseph Ashker and Shafika Ashker, was officially the first Niagara Falls casualty at Pearl Harbor, after being wounded at Wheeler Field. He was twenty-three years old during the incident and had enlisted in the United States Air Corps in 1939, after attending Trott Vocational School. At first, he was sent to a port on the American Pacific coast. In just a short time, he was transferred to Hawaii. His brother, Joseph Ashker, served with the Army Air Corps, too, but was stationed at Mitchell Field on Long Island.

Ashker vividly recalled his experience at Pearl Harbor for a news story in the *Niagara Falls Gazette* twenty years later.[23] "What's going on? I said and my buddy answered: It's the Japs you fool!"[24] Ashker was going to chow when the attack came. He was stationed at Wheeler Field, the first area targeted by the Japanese. A five-hundred-pound bomb hit his barracks, injuring him and killing many others. He had been only "a foot from death," he said.[25] The impact of the bomb blasted him out of his shoes and hurled him into the mess hall. When he finally came to, he crawled through a hole in the wall, only to see bullets whirring past his head. He eventually found his way back to his shoes, and less than a foot away were the bodies of two young soldiers. He ended up in the dispensary with a four-inch gash in his head, a deep cut at the back of his neck and broken ribs. But he was one of the lucky ones, he mentioned, after describing the other hopelessly wounded men he saw that day.

On May 16, 1943, Sergeant Ashker was a guest speaker for the "I Am an American Day" observance held in the auditorium at Gaskill Junior High School. The nearly seven hundred Niagara Falls residents who had recently become naturalized American citizens listened as Ashker passionately declared, "The army is depending upon you folks back home to provide the supplies which are needed to carry on this battle against the Axis. I know you won't let the army—or the other armed forces down."[26]

On December 6, 2011, the *Niagara Falls Gazette* published a story about veteran and Pearl Harbor survivor Yeoman John H. Auchu after his daughter, Linda Sheldon, discovered her father's thirteen-page eyewitness account of his experience during the event. She said it had amazed her to read and to actually be able to perceive what he felt, heard and saw at Pearl Harbor on December 7, 1941.[27]

Linda Sheldon points to a photo of her father, John Auchu, who is sitting next to his brother. *Courtesy James Neiss,* Niagara Falls Gazette, *December 6, 2011.*

Auchu served as a United States Navy yeoman and was stationed on board the USS *Helena* at Ford Island, located in the middle of Pearl Harbor. He had grown up in the Village of LaSalle, on Seventy-Ninth Street, and joined the navy shortly after graduating from LaSalle High School in 1936. He graduated from Niagara University and later taught Latin at the Niagara Wheatfield School District. His account recalled that he was getting ready for church when the first bombs fell. To be precise, he was "combing his hair and preparing to go topside for Mass when he heard two very loud explosions in quick succession."[28] He assumed a plane had crash-landed. But the explosions continued. He saw the "red suns" on the wings of the planes and knew, at once, that something terrible was happening.

> *And then another explosion—louder....Planes started whizzing over the ship—very low and very fast. I quickly stepped over and stuck my head out the open porthole and looked up. There directly above me (and not very far above), I see three planes directly behind one another and travelling very fast. On the undersides of the wings of each I see two very large and very*

red circles. I pull my head back in and start to say something to my "striker" when the loud speaker system clicks on and I recognize the hurried voice of the officer of the deck saying words which I shall never forget: "All hands, man your battle stations. Break out service ammunition. The Japanese are attacking Ford Island."[29]

His own ship, the *Helena*, was torpedoed, and he found himself suddenly injured. He could hear gunfire and antiaircraft guns. The *Helena*, known as the U.S. fleet's "Fightin'est Ship," survived the attack of December 7, 1941, and in time became the first ship to receive the Navy Unit Commendation, awarded for distinguished action against the enemy with outstanding heroism. Unfortunately, the *Helena* was sunk in July 1943 in Kula Gulf. Auchu was on board when a bomb split it open. He and the other survivors awaited rescue in rafts while sharks circled and hunted them. He was one of the last to be rescued by the USS *Radford*.

Private First Class James A. Rader was also able to share his personal account of the attack on Pearl Harbor. "I wanted to pray but I couldn't think of any prayers that I knew," he said.[30]

Rader had been at a departure party until 4:30 a.m. on the morning of December 7 and had barely slept, for it was about 8:00 a.m. when he was thrown out of his bed and ordered out of the barracks. He saw terrible things that day: the wounded, the dead, buildings on fire, boats in flames and the majority of the hangars destroyed. Eventually, a bomb exploded nearby, and he received shrapnel in his left shoulder and right hip. At the field hospital, when the shrapnel was removed, he was offered whiskey to dull his pain. Another bomb exploded, sending clouds of debris onto the patients and staff.

Rader received the Purple Heart and several campaign ribbons designating his participation in the Asiatic and Pacific campaigns. He enlisted on December 26, 1939, and served much of his time in the Pacific. His most important message to the people of Niagara Falls was "to send constant, lengthy letters. Especially welcome are those descriptive ones with a lot of hometown news about the street, the kids, neighbors and that gal Sal."[31]

Other servicemen from Niagara Falls present at Pearl Harbor that fateful day included Staff Sergeant Roy T. Pope, Sergeant Anthony Pelsoni and Sergeant Joseph Golba. Pope was wounded during the attack and was awarded the Purple Heart at a special ceremony at Hickam Field for his "meritorious acts of essential service shown during the December 7th attack."[32] Pelsoni was a gunner and pilot in the army air forces. He served

Sergeant Joseph Golba at Pearl Harbor. *Courtesy Stephanie Golba.*

four years in the Pacific theater of war and flew forty missions. He bombed Tarawa in the Gilbert Islands, Guadalcanal, Iwo Jima, the Marshall Islands and Saipan. He was awarded the Distinguished Flying Cross and three air medals. In an interview with the *Niagara Falls Gazette* on December 3, 1961, Pelsoni said, "We didn't know what was coming off when it happened. There was so much smoke, it looked like nighttime."[33] Golba had arrived at the Hawaiian Islands in January 1940 to join a Coast Artillery unit charged with the defense of Pearl Harbor. He was also present during the attacks. He remained at Pearl Harbor for three years as a gun commander of an antiaircraft artillery battery.

Mrs. Blankenhorn, formerly of Niagara Falls, was one of the first Niagarans mentioned in the *Niagara Falls Gazette* after the attack occurred. The former Ruth LeMasters was the wife of First Lieutenant R.D. Blankenhorn, of the Quartermaster Corps, stationed in Hawaii. Although she was not in the heat of the battle, she was able to see the aerial combat and hear the explosions of the bombs from her home in Honolulu. She returned to Niagara Falls in January 1942 to visit with family and described her experiences to the newspaper.[34]

Another Niagara Falls woman who survived Pearl Harbor, along with her three children, was Mrs. Howard R. Fellenz. Patsy Fellenz, the wife of Lieutenant Howard R. Fellenz, arrived in Niagara Falls on January 5, 1942, after being evacuated from Hawaii with another 850 wives and children of army, air corps and navy men. Her husband had been called to active duty and was assigned to Hickam Field in November 1940. They loved the mild temperatures and the beautiful scenery, but it all became a nightmare on the morning of December 7, 1941. Mrs. Fellenz awakened to the tremendous roar of airplanes around 8:00 a.m., but she really did not make much more of it, as she was used to airplanes flying overhead at all hours of the day. She was not worried at all until she noticed the columns of smoke rising from Pearl Harbor. She made her way to a neighbor's house, and as she crossed the street, she saw a plane dive and sprinkle machine gun bullets nearby. She also saw the insignia of the Rising Sun on the planes. When she realized what was taking place, she ran back home for her children and brought them to a safer dwelling, where she and another mother lay on the floor for over three hours with their children under them while bombs burst all around the neighborhood.

Patsy received the evacuation notice on Christmas morning. The Fellenz family celebrated for just a short time and then made it out to the ship that would take Mrs. Fellenz and her children home by noon. Her great praise was for the Red Cross workers who helped the exhausted passengers. They took charge of the children and even provided emergency clothing, as most of the evacuees had not been able to bring winter-appropriate clothing. Upon arriving in Niagara Falls, she and her children stayed for some time with Mrs. Gordon Harrison at 1653 Linwood Avenue.[35] Captain Howard Fellenz, whose father had served in the army during World War I, was awarded the Purple Heart for gallantry in action at Pearl Harbor.

At least one Niagara Falls man who was lucky enough to live through Pearl Harbor sadly did not make it to see the end of the war. The Ross family never gave up hope that their son, Sergeant Thomas E. Ross, would one day come home to Niagara Falls. A survivor of Pearl Harbor, he was cited for decorations for his activity during the attack and in patrolling duties after the attack. He was a member of the crew of the first bomber to leave the field after the strike. Eighteen of his associates in the barracks were killed.

Ross was reported missing in action in June 1942, when a bomber plane carrying him and Major General Tinker, a commander in the United States Army Air Force, vanished during the Midway encounter with the Japanese. Before his disappearance, he had been stationed at various army flying fields, where he served as an instructor for radio crews. He only recently had been sent back into action when he was lost.

By October 1943, the army had updated his status to killed in action. His parents, Mr. and Mrs. Ross, received the Silver Star posthumously awarded to their son from Brigadier General Richard C. Coupland, air ordnance officer, in Washington, D.C. Ross never did make it home.

MAY THEY NOT HAVE DIED IN VAIN

Just as armed troops were descending on the city of Niagara Falls, setting up machine guns at various danger points, and as all the world stood poised for total war, a group of individuals with the Hermes Club, an affiliate of Hermes International, met at the famed Cataract House. The Cataract House, originally built in 1825, was one of Niagara Falls' grandest hotels, offering unequalled views of the Niagara rapids. Some of the world's greatest men and women had stopped here for a rest. The guestbooks contain the signatures of historic figures such as Abraham Lincoln, Ulysses S. Grant, Jenny Lind, Franklin D. Roosevelt, King Edward VIII and King George V. On December 8, 1941, the Hermes Club meeting was hosted by local musician Alfred DiRocco. DiRocco, an accomplished pianist, had studied music in Italy and with the finest musicians in the United States. This particular evening's program included the following musical selections: "Clair de Lune" by Debussy, "Sevilla" by Albeniz, "Liebestraume" by Liszt and "Rhapsody in Blue" by Gershwin.

President William M. McMahon led a moving tribute "to the memory of those killed in Japan's undeclared attack on the American outposts in the

The Cataract House Hotel, circa 1940s. *Courtesy Niagara Falls Public Library.*

Pacific."[36] The club members stood in silence for thirty seconds. "May they not have died in vain," McMahon concluded.[37]

The new war was suddenly invading every aspect of life at home and abroad. Niagarans were opening their hearts. They were praising the wounded and the dead and preparing for the worst.

CANADIAN CAMARADERIE

As the bond between the United States and Canada has always been quite strong in Niagara Falls, due to the fact that only a river divides the two nations, perhaps it didn't come as much of a surprise that the Canadians would voice their sympathy and cast their support for the United States following the declaration of war and the surprise attack on Pearl Harbor. When a letter arrived from Major Isabel Fraser, commanding officer of the Women's Auxiliary Service Patrol (WASP) at Niagara Falls, Ontario, a "feeling of oneness, union of effort and joint responsibility" was expressed.[38] The letter was addressed to Betty J. Harries, commanding officer of the Niagara Falls Women's Air Raid Wardens Service Force, and said: "And we across the river will be beside you shoulder to shoulder, for our cities will share whatever trials lie ahead. There will be no glory for any of us; there may be death for some of us. What happens to the individual is of no great consequence so long as freedom lives....Good luck to you all. Thumbs up!"[39]

The American and Canadian women's groups had actually been working alongside each other for quite some time and had been guests of each other on various occasions involving training sessions. The Americans had watched their Canadian counterparts drill and conduct classes and had been entertained by them. They were also present at a very special moment when the WASPs were presented with their own and the king's colors. Major Fraser, in turn, was present in Niagara Falls when their American comrades received their colors.

Canada had declared war on the Third Reich on September 10, 1939. About 1.6 million Canadians served in the armed forces. Many were of various ethnic backgrounds and connected by blood and through friendships with their neighbors across the border in the United States.

I Will Give My Allegiance

In the first harried moments at the outbreak of war, it was declared that there were no Japanese people in the Niagara Falls area.[40] However, that was not entirely true, for there actually was one lone Japanese resident of Niagara Falls: Theodore (Tsuyeazi) T. Kondo. Kondo was quite well known around the city. In fact, he had operated a photographic studio in Niagara Falls for twenty-one years before that fateful day in 1941. He had come to the United States from Japan in 1906 as a student in hope of studying medicine at the University of Washington. He planned to return to Japan after receiving his degree. Insufficient funds caused him to change his course of study, and tragedy struck at the same time. His entire family back in Japan perished during the great influenza epidemic of 1918. His return to Japan seemed impossible. In the meantime, he started taking pictures and came to realize that photography was his passion and would be his life's new work. He decided to change his plans and, in 1914, graduated from the Illinois College of Photography at Effingham. He started a partnership with a

A photo by Kondo Studio of Carmela Carlo. *Courtesy Lewiston Public Library.*

classmate in Pennsylvania and soon after met the woman who would become his wife, Mary LeVant De Long. They honeymooned in Niagara Falls and were thunderstruck by the beauty of the great waterfall. It was then that they decided this was where they would spend the rest of their lives. Three years later, they opened a studio at 108 Falls Street. They also kept a studio at 343 Third Street. In 1937, they opened a new studio at 1120 Main Street. Niagarans flocked to Kondo's studio, for his work was impeccable.

On December 9, 1941, Kondo issued a statement to the *Niagara Falls Gazette* regarding the strike at Pearl Harbor. He revealed a personal story of his Japanese heritage and explained his feelings about the situation at hand. He found the actions of the Japanese government to be "both unfortunate and foolhardy" and an act of "national suicide."[41] He went further to state that he looked on the United States as a "benefactor."[42] He was grateful to be a resident of Niagara Falls, and he reached out for the support of the community, for he knew that times would not be easy for Japanese Americans considering the current state of affairs:

> *I want to make it clear to the people of Niagara Falls that for the last twenty-one years I have been a resident of your community and I have conducted myself in a manner which has, I am sure, earned your respect for both myself and my family. I have tried to be one of you....America is my adopted land by choice and to America I will give my allegiance.*[43]

During World War II, he took many pictures of servicemen. "I was more than ever impressed by the need to produce the best possible pictures of the boys who were going off to war," he said.[44] He was so well respected by people in the area that he was not investigated by federal authorities. "The people of this city were wonderful to me," he noted during an interview. "'You don't have to worry, Mr. Kondo,' they told me. 'We're your friends and we understand how tough this war must be on you.'"[45]

By the end of his thirty-eight-year career, he estimated that he had taken close to fifty thousand photographs. Barred from citizenship for some time due to the Oriental Exclusion Act, he finally became a United States citizen on June 22, 1953. It was a joyous occasion for him, and his wife surprised him with a brand-new Cadillac.[46]

ENEMY ALIENS

Almost immediately, "enemy aliens" were rounded up across the United States. German, Italian and Japanese individuals were suddenly seen as possible dangerous elements. On December 9, 1941, it was reported that about four hundred Germans and Italians and over one thousand Japanese were arrested due to a presidential proclamation "to apprehend those Axis nationals who were believed dangerous to the nation's peace and security."[47] Locally, it was reported on December 12, 1941, that twenty-nine individuals were apprehended in the western New York area.[48]

It was believed that several Niagara Falls residents were on this list. A few months later, in March 1942, over twenty homes in the Niagara Falls area were searched by the FBI, and contraband was removed. Seizures included "emblems of German nationalistic societies."[49] The former immigration building located at Depot Avenue and Ninth Street was to be used as a detention center for enemy aliens.

NEW YEAR'S MESSAGE TO THE PEOPLE OF NIAGARA FALLS, DECEMBER 1941

The assault at Pearl Harbor on December 7, 1941, changed everything in Niagara Falls and in much of the world at large. It left over two thousand Americans dead and more than one thousand wounded. The United States was suddenly provoked into a world war. Mayor Ernest W. Mirrington Jr., addressed the year's events in a special year-end statement to the citizens of Niagara Falls:

> *The year 1941 has been a year which will take its place as one of the most eventful and important in the history of the entire world. During the past year, our nation has become involved in a total war, the result of which will undoubtedly determine the future welfare of all people. We fight with the champions of freedom against those who would enslave all free men.*[50]

Words like these were inspirational and spurred a nation to action. This was the good fight, and this was the greatest generation.

Chapter 2

MOBILIZATION

Buck Private

When victory is accomplished and the Niagara Falls boys come marching home, to their friends, their families and their city, I hope to be with them, and perhaps then I shall be given another opportunity to serve my community.
—*Mayor Ernest W. Mirrington Jr.*[51]

Just about eighty years before the mayor of Niagara Falls, Ernest W. Mirrington Jr., left for war in 1942, another great Niagara leader left for war as well. Colonel Peter A. Porter, son of one of the city's fathers, similarly joined the ranks of Niagara men during the War of the Rebellion. He led the Eighth New York Heavy Artillery, known as the "Bloody Eighth," through numerous battles and ultimately gave his life at Cold Harbor, Virginia, on June 3, 1864. Over one hundred Niagarans lost their lives in just a few hours. Colonel Porter, who was from a privileged family, had been offered a political position to remove him from the heat of battle. He refused. Instead, he said the following: "I left home in command of a regiment composed mainly of the sons of friends and neighbors committed to my care. I can hardly ask for my discharge while theirs cannot be granted; and I have a strong desire, if alive, to carry back those whom the chances of time and war shall permit to be present, and to account in person for all."[52]

Men with such inclinations toward valor are not common. But twice in Niagara Falls' history, great leaders were poised for action.

Ernest W. Mirrington Jr. was not your typical mayor. A Republican, he took office on January 1, 1940, and officially resigned on December 31,

1942, following his induction into the army. At the time, he was the youngest mayor in the state of New York. He was only thirty-four when he initially took office. He served his time and, in January 1952, was elected mayor of the city of Niagara Falls once again.

By the middle of 1942, it must have seemed as if everyone's sons, husbands, fathers and sweethearts were off to war. It was only a matter of time. And soon, even the mayor of Niagara Falls received his orders.

At first there were questions regarding this situation. Would it even be wise for a city of such vital importance to the war effort to lose its mayor at this critical moment? But Ernest Mirrington was determined to serve his country. On June 13, 1942, he, along with three busloads of other selectees from Niagara Falls, was inducted into the United States Army at the Old Customs House in Buffalo. The mayor led the group of men, which also included Michael J. Harmon, a history instructor at Niagara University, as well as the third son of Mr. and Mrs. Frank L. McAlee of Sixty-Eighth Street, who was now one of three brothers called into the army.

At the recent city council meeting, Mayor Mirrington had been granted a leave of absence and had received well wishes from the council and city employees. Like the other inductees, he was given a physical examination and then transported to Fort Niagara, where he was issued uniforms and officially processed by the army.

The processing of the mayor was not without a touch of humor. Apparently, the joke was on the mayor when he found himself issued the most ridiculous sizes for his clothing allotment. The *Niagara Falls Gazette* had a bit of fun at his expense when describing the sizes the clerk handed him. "They would have made better pillow cases," according to the newspaper.[53] Not to mention the fact that "his trousers encompassed his waistline twice and still left room for a couple of army jeeps to park."[54] Even with this mix-up, Private First Class Mirrington remained acquiescent. But when he found himself fully clothed in his new uniform, which "wasn't even a good makeup for a masquerade,"[55] the mayor burst into laughter.

In the end, the *Niagara Falls Gazette* was proud to note that "he took everything good naturedly and laughed aloud when he realized he was the butt of a practical joke concocted by his friends at Fort Niagara."[56] However, the most comical aspect of this story may have been that the mayor was actually prepared for such a situation and had even brought a package of safety pins as "an emergency measure."[57]

"I'll sure remember this if I live to be a thousand," he quipped at the end.[58]

He's in the Army Now

Photo by Roy G. Crogan, Gazette Staff Photographer

Private Ernest W. Mirrington, Jr., mayor of Niagara Falls (left), pictured as he left the processing building at Fort Niagara yesterday, accompanied by Lieutenant Sidney Henderson, the post's public relations officer, after being issued his new clothing as a member of Uncle Sam's army.

Mayor Ernest W. Mirrington Jr. joins the army. *From* Niagara Falls Gazette.

Then came a serious moment, for this was a serious time. All jokes aside, he told the reporter that "being in this man's army is really going to do me a lot of good."[59]

Mayor Mirrington was well respected for his service to his country. Upon his first public appearance in uniform, while marching in a parade at Main and Prospect Streets, it was noted that "a continuous roar of applause for the soldier-mayor followed his progress down the line."[60]

NIAGARA IS CALLED TO ACTION

The draft boards in Niagara Falls had begun calling forth men as early as the beginning of 1941 due to the provisions of the Selective Service Act. Three boards had been organized in the city of Niagara Falls by October 1940 and were "functioning smoothly."[61] District 581 included the First, Second, Third, Fourth, Fourteenth and Fifteenth Wards (headquarters located on Buffalo Avenue at LaSalle High School); District 582 included the Fifth, Sixth, Seventh and Ninth Wards (headquarters located at the board of education office building, 607 Walnut Avenue); and District 583 included the Eighth, Tenth, Eleventh, Twelfth and Thirteenth Wards, as well as the town of Niagara (headquarters located on Hyde Park at Gaskill Junior High School). The boards were created in order to decide which young men were eligible for immediate call to service. They would classify registrants by sending out questionnaires to those who registered under the Selective Service Act. The registration cards were numbered at these various district boards. Master numbers were drawn in Washington, D.C., by the secretary of war beginning on October 29, 1940. Young men were urged to register with their respective boards. Those failing to register could be criminally prosecuted as draft dodgers.

A PORTRAIT OF A SELECTEE FROM NIAGARA FALLS: PRIVATE FIRST CLASS ARTHUR E. BARTHEL

Arthur Emil Barthel had come to Niagara Falls from Wheeling, West Virginia, in the late 1930s, like many other men, in search of work. His cousin Mrs. Herman Schmidt had visited family in Wheeling and urged Arthur to come

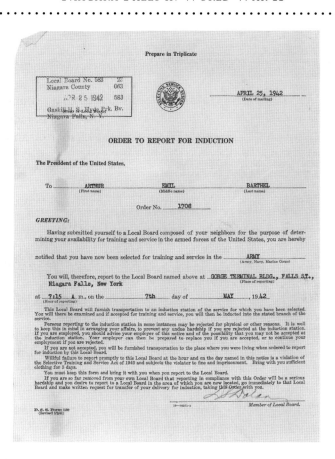

Above: Induction papers for Arthur E. Barthel. *Author's collection.*

Right: Arthur E. Barthel. *Author's collection.*

back to Niagara Falls with her, as jobs were plentiful.[62] He had nothing to lose, so he moved up north and soon after found employment at the Electrometallurgical Company as a chemical furnace tender. He lived with his cousin's family for some time and then roomed as a boarder at 314 Seventy-Sixth Street in LaSalle. On April 25, 1942, the call to action finally came when Local Draft Board No. 583 summoned him to duty at Gaskill Junior High School. He was notified to report to the Gorge Terminal Building at Falls Street at 7:15 a.m. on May 7, 1942. Arthur Barthel was with the first group of the twenty-fifth contingent of selectees called from Niagara Falls. The group was taken by train to the Old Customs House in Buffalo, where they were given complete physical examinations and finally inducted into the army. Following this, the men were returned to Fort Niagara, where they spent three to five days processing into the army. They received their clothing allotments at this time and also underwent a preliminary training. At this point, the men were assigned to various army camps across the United States. Private First Class Arthur E. Barthel was assigned the military occupational specialty of chemical handler (MOS 784) and headed to Barksdale Field in Louisiana, where he attended the Army Air Forces Chemical Training Center and was trained in the use of chemical warfare. He was a member of the 874th Chemical Company at Barksdale. He served with the army air forces for the remainder of the war with the 351st Bomb Squadron at Thorpe Abbots, England.

THE WOMEN'S ARMY AUXILIARY CORPS AND THE WOMEN'S ARMY CORPS

On May 14, 1942, President Franklin Delano Roosevelt signed legislation making it possible for American women to serve in the army beside men in noncombat positions for the first time ever. The women of the Women's Army Auxiliary Corps (WAAC) were the first women, other than nurses, to serve in the ranks of the United States Army. By July 3, 1943, the WAC (Women's Army Corps) Bill was signed into law, converting the WAAC into the regular army. Instead of serving the army, the WAC would be part of the army itself.

More than 150,000 women served in the WAC during World War II. Some WACs went overseas; others stayed stateside. Some performed specialized and secret war work after being assigned to the Office of Strategic Services

(OSS).[63] The only requirements for being a member of the WAC included being a woman between the ages of twenty and forty-nine, being physically fit and having no children under the age of fourteen. By 1944, the army offered a new triple-choice plan for women interested in joining. It would allow the recruits to choose their desired jobs from a list of 239 positions, have their choice of branch of service (army air forces, army ground forces or army service forces) and also have their choice of location for assignment.[64]

Women's Army Corps poster. *From* Niagara Falls Gazette.

The official WAC recruiting station in Niagara Falls was located at 43 West Falls Street, at the chamber of commerce building.

During WAC Recruiting Week, May 11–17, 1944, the motion picture *WAC Recruiting Week* was screened at theaters throughout the city of Niagara Falls. Personnel were on hand to answer any questions and to recruit new members. "What can I do to help with the war? One answer is to join the WACs."[65]

Mayor Stephen A. Lamb proclaimed July 26 through July 29, 1944, WAC Week in Niagara Falls. The importance of the Women's Army Corps was reinforced throughout his proclamation.[66] At the same time, a team of army air forces recruiters from the New York Air Service Guard at Rome had come to Niagara Falls with information and ready to take on new members. They were in desperate need of women who could work the control tower, bring in planes for safe landing, drive jeeps and repair motors. There were large displays of Air Corps equipment in the Beir Brothers display window on Second Street and at Butler's Florist at Main and Third Streets, including a Flying Fortress tire, a bazooka, a "Mae West" life preserver, a "Gibson Girl" radio, a five-man life raft and other items.[67]

The first official ceremony in which women were sworn into the WAC in Niagara Falls took place at Prospect Point, at the brink of Niagara Falls, on November 5, 1943. With the roar of the mighty waterfall setting the scene, Lieutenant Elizabeth Thompson administered the oath of enlistment and Sergeant L. Wienke acted as standard-bearer. Relatives and friends of the women were present as Mayor Eugene C. Butler presented each of the women with a white ribbon on which was painted in black lettering "WAC, Niagara Falls. Niagara Falls is proud to have you represent them as privates in this great army of the United States."[68] True N. Hewitt of the Civilian Recruiting Committee presented the women with brassards that were also stamped WAC, Niagara Falls. "We want your future companions in the WAC to know that you came from Niagara Falls."[69]

Two of the women sworn in that day were Mary and Anne Malensky. They were sisters and had only recently moved to Niagara Falls from Fredericktown, Pennsylvania, in order to work at Bell Aircraft. They were compelled to commit themselves to the service of their country due to the fact that they had brothers and boyfriends in the army and the navy and also because they were of Polish heritage. Mary was sworn in as a WAC, and Anne was sworn in as a WAVE for the United States Navy.

In March 1945, WAC members were honored in a tribute to the women who had "given up the luxuries of home life to join the Women's Army Corps."[70] A

WAC Honor Roll was prepared by the local army recruiting office. It was presented to Mayor Stephen A. Lamb and the commander of the John J. Welch No. 381 American Legion Post. This honor roll was on display in the Beir Brothers display window and then moved to another location. The names listed on this honor roll included Winifred F. Allen, Alice S. Baird, Jean Banes, Stella Bank, Jean L. Bellinger, Mabel Boser, Jane Broadwell, Carmela Carlo, Doris Channing, Irene Chudsin, Rose Cindrish, Dorothy Cruickshank, Caroline Czaplak, Mary Densmore, Dorothy Dolan, Mary Elenski, Nettie Elenski, Mary C. Fowler, Alverda Freeman, Jennie Furri, Patricia

Carmela Carlo, WAC. *Courtesy Lewiston Public Library.*

Gauthier, Margaret Gorman, Mary Hallen, Geraldine Hart, Florence Holody, Ruth Irwin, Mary Jansen, Bernice Jarlenski, Irene Jarlenski, Sylvia Johnson, Dora Jordan, Mildred Jordan, Alyse Kahn, Bernice Klimecko, Catherine Lewin, Jenni Lucci, Bernice Maday, Mary Malensky, Mary McDougall, Betty Meckley, Margaret Merrill, Bernice Mittelstead, Mabel Nelson, Mary Pullano, Ethel Reynolds, Rosalie Sceusam, Norma Shaw, Mary Shay, Bernice Skutas, Josephine Smiadala, Gretchen Smith, Frances Thorne, Vernell Walden, Mary Welch, Ruth Welzmiller, Helen Woida and Agnes Young.

A PORTRAIT OF A WAC:
PRIVATE FIRST CLASS INDIANA HUNT-MARTIN

In November 2014, a Niagara Falls woman who had served in the first female African American battalion was finally recognized for her service with the Women's Army Corps during World War II. In a ceremony held at AMVETS

Medallion Post 13 in Buffalo, New York, at Riverside, she was presented with the Women's Army Corps Service Medal, the European-African-Middle Eastern Campaign Medal, the World War II Victory Medal and the Honorable Service Lapel Button by Congressman Brian Higgins. It was only days before the sixty-nine-year anniversary of her honorable discharge.

Private First Class Indiana Hunt-Martin moved to Niagara Falls with her family in 1926. She was born in Georgia. Following her graduation from Niagara Falls High School in 1940, she found it was difficult for African American women to find jobs. For a time, she cleaned houses. She also worked in Lewiston picking peaches. She had heard about the Women's Army Corps and thought that since her brother was also serving in the army, why couldn't she? On September 15, 1944, she joined the WAC.

She encountered a great deal of segregation during her trip to Fort Oglethorpe, Georgia, for WAC training. Outside the army post, there were

The 6888th Central Postal Directory Battalion, February 15, 1945, somewhere in England. Major Charity E. Adams and Captain Abbie N. Campbell inspect the first contingent of African American members of the Women's Army Corps assignment to overseas service. Private First Class Indian Hunt is the second woman in the second row from the right side. *Courtesy National Archives.*

places where African Americans were not allowed to go. There were separate restrooms and drinking fountains, and African Americans were supposed to sit at the back of the bus.

She was a member of the 6888th Central Postal Directory Battalion. It was the first female African American battalion in the army and also the only all-female battalion to be sent overseas.

The trip across the ocean was terrifying. There was the threat of German U-boats and submarines. She was deployed at first to Birmingham, England, where she worked on sorting through all the mail from the European front. Often her work was in readdressing mail so that it made it to the correct destination. With the men moving around the continent, sometimes locations were difficult to pinpoint for mail delivery.

When the war ended, she was sent to France, where she saw much of the devastation—and there was more mail to be sorted as well.

Finally, she returned to the United States, to Niagara Falls, where she found a job with the New York State Labor Department. She became the first African American officeworker in the city of Niagara Falls.

Indiana's medals were long overdue. They were probably neglected, she said, due to the fact that her surname changed.[71] She was very pleased when they were finally presented to her, almost seventy years later.

WAVES and SPARS

The WAVES (Women Accepted for Volunteer Emergency Service) were the women's branch of the United States Naval Reserve. They were established on July 21, 1942, by the United States Congress and signed into law by President Franklin Delano Roosevelt on July 30, 1942. The creation of the WAVES, who would serve in posts at shore stations, freed up the men in the navy for sea duty.

Ensign Barbara Peck, WAVES, was assigned to the city of Niagara Falls to aid in the recruitment of WAVES. The recruitment office was located in the navy recruitment substation in the post office building on the first and third Mondays of each month, from 9:00 a.m. to 5:00 p.m. Women between the ages of twenty and thirty-five were encouraged to apply.

According to Ensign Peck, "The best way to be true blue, is to get into navy blue."[72]

Some Niagara Falls women joined the WAVES. Paula G. Focazio, the daughter of Mr. and Mrs. John Focazio of 1347 Ontario Avenue, joined in

January 1943. She had graduated from Niagara Falls High School and the Kelley Business Institute and had previously been employed by the Empire Builders Supply Company.

Another young woman who joined the WAVES was Mildred A. Obenhack. The twenty-six-year-old graduate of Niagara Falls High School was the daughter of Mr. and Mrs. Charles P. Obenhack of 953 McKinley Avenue. She had previously been employed as a secretary for the Niagara Falls War Council.

SPARS were also recruited in Niagara Falls during the war. The United States Coast Guard Women's Reserve, better known as SPARS (which is taken from the first letters of their motto, *Semper Paratus*—"Always Ready"), was not an auxiliary unit. Its members received the same pay and ratings as coast guardsmen and were limited in their service only by a congressional decision that they "may not serve afloat or outside the continental limits of the United States."[73]

Lucille Millard joined the SPARS on April 18, 1945. Millard, the daughter of Mr. and Mrs. Allen Millard, resided at 724 Buffalo Avenue. Before joining the SPARS, she was a receptionist and secretary for radio station WHLD.

Chapter 3

WITH THE SERVICES

There were many men and women from Niagara Falls who served in the military during World War II. They fought in the air, on land and on sea. The war brought Niagarans to the other side of the globe. Most made it back home. Some did not.

Much of what has been chronicled of the men and women who served was done so by writers of the *Niagara Falls Gazette*. Betty J. Harries was one of the journalists who, through her regular wartime columns, formed a lifeline between the men and women in uniform and their families at home. She immortalized many of their stories by her countless interviews and through her timeless articles.

From the beginning, Harries accompanied the troops from Niagara Falls to their training stations and shared whatever she saw and experienced in vivid detail with her readers. She often shared humorous stories regarding particular Niagara men with whom she happened to meet up during training. First Sergeant Harrison Wiltse, a mailman from Niagara Falls, actually acted as a mailman for his company by making sure all the men were never without stamps. Private Frank Krell kept himself occupied in his downtime by collecting a menagerie of pets. As far as Harries knew, he had a kitten, a dog, a few moles, a turtle and a small garter snake.

On one occasion, she was present for a mock attack during a training session. She concluded her story by proudly mentioning that our Niagara Falls boys had all survived the games and were heading back to the camp. Soon after, they were to leave for their real homes in Niagara Falls—but just for a short

Left: Betty J. Harries, wartime *Niagara Falls Gazette* correspondent. *Author's collection.*

Below: Niagara Falls men training at Camp Wheeler, Georgia. *Author's collection.*

time. They would then be sent off to wherever they would be needed. Harries knew that there were many uncertainties, but even so, "you may be sure that the Niagara Falls companies will be ready," she assured everyone.[74]

Betty J. Harries wrote several regular columns that, at times, took up two entire pages. These included: "Women in War Work," "With the Services,"

"Up in the Air," "On the American Front," "News of Niagara Falls Boys in Uncle Sam's Uniform" and "On the Northern Front." She was also very active on the homefront. She was an officer with the air raid wardens, as well as the founder of the Service Force, a volunteer effort to maintain and operate several centers for servicemen in Niagara Falls. The "Hut" was one of the more popular locations and located initially at 447–49 Third Street; in March 1944, it was relocated to 466 Third Street.

It was not always easy for Harries. She was often the only female correspondent. Some of the other male correspondents and army officials did not treat her as they treated the men. She was aware of this fact and wrote about it. She said that the men were "polite, kind and courteous to the utmost" but went on to add that the truth was, they just were "not ready for a Nellie Bly."[75] They were "grand," and without their assistance, she admitted that she could not have had her stories; however, she was tired of the limitations that she faced simply because she was a woman. "It was 'no' to having a tent to sleep in. It was 'no' to going out with the troops on bivouacs."[76] There were too many *nos*. Even as she was often the only woman at camp—such as at the Plattsburgh camps, where the headline read, "Betty Is Lone Girl with 52,000 Troops Engaged in 'Battle'"—she foresaw a future filled with female correspondents.[77] She wrote in her column the following words concerning the predicament in which she and other female writers found themselves:

> *They've got to face the fact that, while there are only one or two of us around now, as long as this army carries on, more and more women reporters are going to be coming around. And they won't just be interested in what the heroes eat, what housing accommodations they have, or what suitable clothing. They're going to demand the same rights as their male colleagues....They just want to be allowed to do the same as any other fellow newsman. And that's not asking much.*[78]

IN UNIFORM

Private First Class Victor Ventresca

Victor Ventresca was born on April 18, 1917, in Torre Dei Nolfi, Italy, and came to the United States in 1929. He entered the service on January 24, 1941,

Your Country needs you

NOW !

ENLIST TODAY

Your Regular Army is calling for volunteers!

Men between 18 and 35 are needed for all of the Arms and Services.

The Air Force wants thousands of young men, *immediately*. Training schools are ready now for large numbers of Air Mechanics, Aerial Photographers and other specialists.

AVIATION CADETS

Many thousands of aviation cadets, 20 to 26 years of age, inclusive, are needed to become flying officers as bombardiers, navigators and pilots.

You can help in building the world's most powerful Air Force, and in the necessary expansion of the Regular Army.

ACTION IS NEEDED NOW!

Your country has decided. The treacherous attack on America has aroused the United States as nothing else could.

Your Army is ready. Call at the nearest Army Recruiting Station for advice. You will be given full information on how you can serve your country best — how you can defend that freedom which is your birthright.

"Let's go! U.S.A. Keep 'em Flying!"

U.S. ARMY RECRUITING SERVICE

FEDERAL BLDG., NIAGARA FALLS, N. Y.

Enlist today! U.S. Army wartime recruitment poster. *From* Niagara Falls Gazette.

and served on the Pacific front. He was part of General MacArthur's victorious return to the Philippines. Ventresca's service afforded him a direct route to American citizenship, which he obtained on March 10, 1947. He was the son of Mr. and Mrs. Angelo Ventresca of 827 Nineteenth Street.

Sergeant Isaac "Jack" Martinez

Jack Martinez, the son of Mr. and Mrs. Victor Martinez, was inducted into the army on January 24, 1941. He left with one of the largest groups of prewar selectees (which also included Victor Ventresca). He served in the army infantry, Twenty-Seventh Division, M Company, in Hawaii for two years. Due to illness, he was sent to San Francisco and then honorably discharged. His brothers who were old enough also served during World War II: Michael, Victor, Manuel and Gabriel. His brother Joe could not serve because of his missing fingers, which were lost coupling boxcars while working at Dupont.

Private First Class Matthew Eden

On December 28, 1944, Private Matthew Eden was wounded in action in Luxembourg. Born in

Victor Ventresca, U.S. Army. *Courtesy the Ventresca family.*

Isaac "Jack" Martinez, U.S. Army Infantry. *Courtesy the Martinez family.*

Private Matthew Eden, of Niagara Falls and formerly of Glasgow, Scotland, takes the oath during the swearing-in ceremony in which 150 aliens become U.S. citizens in Britain, May 28, 1943. *Author's collection.*

Glasgow, Scotland, he came to Niagara Falls in the 1930s. He worked at the U.S.L. Battery Corporation before his induction into the army. He was awarded a Purple Heart and three Bronze Stars for valor in the European Theater.

Private First Class Thomas Kane and Private First Class Andrew Kane

Brothers Thomas and Andrew Kane both served in the army during World War II. Thomas was with the 1019th Ordnance Company. He began overseas duty in November 1943 and served in the campaigns at New Guinea, Bismarck Archipelago and the Philippines. He had attended Trott Vocational School before the war.

Andrew Kane served for four years with the 397th Military Police Battalion in France.

Private First Class Charles A. Scime

Charles A. Scime served with the United States Army, 107th Medical Battalion, in the Asiatic Pacific Theater of Operations as a medic. In March 1945, as the Battle of Luzon raged in the Philippines, in the midst of combat, he wrote to his parents and told them "not to worry" and that he was "ok." He went on to explain details of his experiences on the Pacific front.[79] He was wounded at Luzon and received two Bronze Battle Stars and a Purple Heart. He was the son of Mr. and Mrs. Vito Scime of 1418 Robinson Court.

Top: Thomas J. Kane in New Guinea, 1944. *Courtesy Beverly Bidak.*

Right: Andrew Kane in France, 1942. *Courtesy Beverly Bidak.*

Corporal John (Jack) Vincent O'Connor

Jack enlisted in the army in June 1943 and served as a paratrooper with the 101st Airborne. He went overseas in November 1944 and served in England, France and Belgium. He was wounded at the Battle of the Bulge, suffering shrapnel wounds. He was awarded the Purple Heart, a Presidential Unit Citation, a medal from France and a medal from Belgium.

In 2014, just a few days after Veterans' Day, Jack was reunited with his comrade-in-arms Richard Olson, whom he served alongside. They spoke on the telephone and corresponded through mail until Richard's death shortly after.

Private Arthur Gallo

Born in Rochester, New York, Arthur Gallo married a woman from Niagara Falls, Rose Falsetti. He was stationed at Fort

Top: Charles A. Scime. *Courtesy Charleen Scime.*

Left: John "Jack" O'Connor. *Courtesy the O'Connor family.*

Richard Olson and John "Jack" O'Connor, 101st Airborne, in France. *Courtesy the O'Connor family.*

Arthur Gallo and Rose Falsetti. *Courtesy Kathy Gallo Abbondanza.*

Dix, New Jersey, during their engagement. Rose was the daughter of Mr. and Mrs. Guy Falsetti of Thirteenth Street. Arthur was the son of Mr. and Mrs. Arthur Gallo of Rochester.

FIGHTING FAMILIES

Niagara Falls saw many brothers and sisters in the various branches of our fighting forces. Some families volunteered two or three of their sons and

Clockwise from top left: Patricia Palumbo's father was away with the army during World War II, but he kept in touch through the mail. *Courtesy Patricia Palumbo DiNieri*; Private First Class Anthony Palumbo. *Courtesy Patricia Palumbo DiNieri*; "Hello Honey, Hoping you're in the best of health and back to school again. Daddy misses you very much and hopes you are a very good girl with mother and also in school. God bless you. Always yours, Daddy." *Courtesy Patricia Palumbo DiNieri*.

daughters to the military. Some volunteered four or five. Betty J. Harries, *Niagara Falls Gazette* staffer, shared their stories with her readers.

Mr. and Mrs. Frank Cortese, of 713 Seventeenth Street, had four sons in the service during World War II. Corporal Frank Cortese Jr., previously an employee at the Empire Building Supply Company, joined the army on June 12, 1941. He was stationed in North Africa. Private First Class Anthony Cortese was drafted in January 1943. He was formerly employed by Union Carbide and served with the Quartermaster Division in Los Angeles, California. Private First Class John Cortese worked for the Vanadium Corporation before entering the service in March 1942. He was a medic wounded in action at Anzio during the Sicilian invasion. He was awarded a Purple Heart. Alfred Cortese, EM, second class, volunteered with the United States Navy on February 28, 1942. He was stationed in the South Pacific. He was well known in Niagara Falls as a local athlete. He had graduated from Trott Vocational School and worked for the Kimberly-Clark Corporation before his enlistment.

Perhaps the largest family group from Niagara Falls serving in World War II was the Carlo family. Five brothers and one sister, the children of Mr. and Mrs. John Carlo of 432 Twenty-Sixth Street, each volunteered. Sergeant Carmela Carlo served with the WAC at Orlando, Florida. Sergeant Samuel Carlo served with a military police detachment in Italy. Sergeant Dominick Carlo was attached to a personnel division at Lakeland, Florida. Private Orlando Carlo served with an antiaircraft division in the Philippines. Private First Class Ubaldo Carlo served with an engineer division in Belgium. Private First Class Olympio Carlo, the last of the siblings to be called into service, was with the army in France.

LETTERS HOME

Many of Niagara's youngest spent the war years without their fathers. Thankfully, the mail delivered regular messages to little Patricia Palumbo. Her father, Anthony Palumbo, served with the army in Europe. Her mother, Amy (Ciambrone) Palumbo, worked as an auxiliary policewoman and guard at the Carborundum plant. Pat remembers the war years and has kept her father's letters.

Chapter 4

TRAGEDIES

On August 15, 1945, *the Niagara Falls Gazette* published its list of Niagara Falls casualties.[80] According to its account, the "price of victory" included the following (exclusive of wounded):

Died in service: 340
Prisoners of war: 83
Missing in action: 61

It was reported, however, that since the list was compiled, fifty POWs had been liberated. Five service members had also been found safe. Publication of a list of the wounded would not have been possible, as it would have required too much space. The war wounded of Niagara Falls ran into the thousands.

It is difficult to look upon the names, addresses and theaters of war for these men who paid the highest price. Imagine the horror for families such as LaSalle's Batarlas, who, while making final plans for the funeral of their son Ensign John A. Batarla, twenty-five, at St. John de LaSalle Church, received a telegram notifying them that another son, Private First Class Francis M. Batarla, United States Marine Corps, had been killed in action. Two other brothers also served.

Death did not always come with glory. Private First Class Harold Chateauneuf, of 407 Ninth Street, died in a POW camp. His family had held out for his survival for three and a half years, only to receive the dreaded notification that he was one of our dead. Chateauneuf had served with General MacArthur's forces on Bataan. He was captured and endured the infamous "death march" to a prison camp in Luzon. Sometime afterward, he was transferred to another camp in Japan, where he died.

There were many German Niagarans who fought in the war as well. Fritz Ries was born in Bavaria, Germany, and arrived in Niagara Falls in 1930. He worked for the Kimberly Clark Corporation and resided on Woodlawn Avenue until he was inducted into the army in August 1942. He had also been a member of the Niagara Falls Liederkranz Society. He fought in the African and Sicilian campaigns and died in action in Italy on October 18, 1943.

Some survived the greatest of ordeals, yet death still found them. Sergeant Joseph Germele, of 1122 Linwood Avenue, was awarded the Silver Star for gallantry in action in the Tunisian campaign. According to the citation that accompanied his medal, he had found himself

> *completely surrounded by the enemy. He refused to give up and destroyed an enemy anti-tank gun at very close range. When the gun's personnel withdrew into inaccessible and concealed fox holes where they could not be reached by tank fire, [he] unhesitatingly dismounted from his tank and armed with a sub-machine gun and hand grenades, killed or captured all of the members of the gun crew.*[81]

His fearless performance earned him the highest praise. Unfortunately, following this incident, he was stricken with leukemia. He was sent to the Veteran's Hospital in Batavia, where he died, and his body was returned to Niagara Falls.

Technical Sergeant Anthony J. Paonessa, the son of Mr. and Mrs. Joseph Paonessa of 546 Eighteenth Street, was a radio operator–gunner on a B-24 Liberator bomber with the Fifteenth Army Air Force. He earned a Distinguished Unit Citation, a Good Conduct Medal, an Air Medal and two Oak Leaf Clusters. Before the war, Paonessa had been employed by Bell Aircraft. He entered the army in February 1943. He completed twenty-eight missions in total and was first reported missing in action over Italy after his plane went down in December 1944. He was buried in a military cemetery in Florence, Italy.

Sergeant Daniel Lucarini, the son of Mr. and Mrs. Fred Lucarini, served with the Fortieth Bomber Squadron, Sixth Bomber Group, VH. He was with crew #4008 on a minelaying mission in March 1945 over the Shimonoseki

Left: Technical Sergeant Anthony J. Paonessa. *Courtesy Marcia Buzzelli*; *Right*: Sergeant Daniel Lucarini. *Courtesy the Lucarini family*.

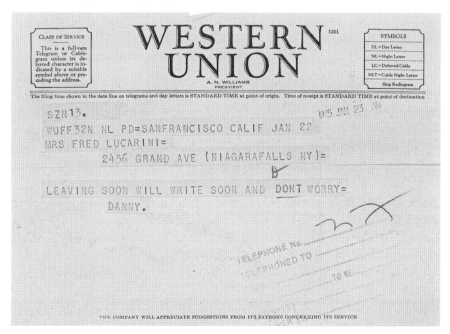

The last message from Sergeant Daniel Lucarini: "Leaving soon. Will write soon and don't worry—Danny." *Courtesy the Lucarini family*.

Straits. They were last heard by radio flying over Kyushu with one engine out. The entire crew was reported missing in action on March 28, 1945. The War Department entertained hopes that the men had survived. On March 29, 1946, the Lucarini family received notification that his status had been changed to killed in action. He is commemorated on the Tablets of the Missing at Honolulu Memorial Cemetery in Hawaii.

On May 27, 1945, at Wright Field in Dayton, Ohio, Captain William C. Glasgow, one of Niagara Falls' most popular pilots, crashed to his death during a war bond rally attended by more than seventy thousand people. His XP-55 Curtiss-Ascender struck an automobile when it crashed, killing four additional individuals. An infant child who was a passenger miraculously survived.

Captain Glasgow, the son of Mr. and Mrs. William C. Glasgow of 1415 Twenty-Seventh Street, had joined the U.S. Army Air Forces in January 1942. He served for one year with the 106th Artillery. He served as a member of the 85th Fighter Squadron of the Western Desert Air Force and had survived through the heaviest fighting in the Mediterranean theater of war. He was reported missing in action in December 1943, after parachuting to the ground and being taken prisoner by the Germans. He was badly wounded but managed to escape and make his way back to his unit. He was awarded the Silver Star for this feat. Glasgow was a veteran of eighty combat missions over enemy territory. His valor on the field also earned him a Distinguished Flying Cross, an Air Medal with six clusters and many other medals and citations.

Captain Glasgow's funeral at Oakwood Cemetery in Niagara Falls was attended by many distinguished airmen and pilots who came from afar to pay their respects. A firing squad from Fort Niagara fired a volley over his grave while a bugler from Wright Field sounded taps.

It is not uncommon for soldiers to look toward the possibility that they might not return home to their loved ones. One soldier from Niagara Falls, Corporal Harry Mokhiber, the son of Mr. and Mrs. Edward Mokhiber of 1513 Lockport Street, wrote a farewell letter, which was to remain unopened until his death, and entrusted it to his sister. After notification of his death in Belgium on April 22, 1945, due to pneumonia and complications from a ruptured appendix, the family opened the letter and shared the contents with the readers of the *Niagara Falls Gazette*. He wrote of many things. The letter could have been from anyone's son or brother. He had hoped that the letter would ultimately be read by himself to his family after the war had been won, but he did not make it to the end. He

Above: Captain Glasgow. *Courtesy the Glasgow family.*

Right: The memorial service for Technical Sergeant James F. Woodcock. *From* Niagara Falls Gazette.

had survived the D-Day invasion with the U.S. Army Corps of Engineers but did not survive a bout of appendicitis. "I don't want you all to feel bad because I gave my life but I want you to be proud of me. I want you to know that I died fighting," he wrote.

The first deceased soldier to be transported back to Niagara Falls for reburial after having been interred in a foreign cemetery was Technical Sergeant James F. Woodcock. Although many others had died before Woodcock, he was the first to come home in this manner. The city decided that a tribute would be made to all Niagara men who had given the ultimate sacrifice overseas upon the arrival of Woodcock's body. His body arrived in a flag-draped coffin at the New York Central Depot railroad station on November 1, 1944. It was met by the family, an honor guard of local veterans, city officials, civic leaders and hundreds of Niagarans. From the depot, it was taken by hearse up Third Street and then along Main Street to city hall, where a solemn memorial service took place. His body lay in state for several hours at city hall before it was taken to its final resting place.

Technical Sergeant James F. Woodcock. *Courtesy the Woodcock family.*

Sergeant Woodcock, the son of Mr. and Mrs. James Woodcock of 6814 Buffalo Avenue, was first inducted into the army on May 12, 1941. He received his pilot's training at Kelly, Randolph and Garner Fields in Texas. He was with the Seventy-Second Liaison Squadron and then became the flight leader of the Nineteenth Liaison Squadron. He spent time in India and China.

On July 27, 1944, Woodcock was killed in an airplane accident over China. His younger brother, Harold, recalled the

Mrs. Mabel Woodcock. *Courtesy the Woodcock family.*

marine who came to their home bearing the dreaded black-rimmed letter from the War Department notifying the family of his death.[82]

Sergeant Woodcock was first buried in a military cemetery in India. His mother, Mabel Woodcock, however, insisted that his body be returned home to Niagara Falls. He was reinterred at Niagara Falls Memorial Park Cemetery. She never forgot him and joined the Niagara Chapter 8 of the Gold Star Mothers organization. Eventually, she became the president. This organization was founded by blood mothers of soldiers killed in war.

Chapter 5

THE HOMEFRONT

The Spirit of Niagara Falls

Niagara Falls, not unlike many other American cities, was called to action during the Second World War. A spirit of generosity and camaraderie brought everyone together for one common cause: victory. With hindsight, it may be difficult to imagine how Niagarans could have so seriously feared the possibility of air raids and military takeover. However, a casual perusal of the wartime newspapers reveals that it was a different world. As cities like London saw forty-three thousand killed at home from Luftwaffe bombings by May 1941, as Paris fell, as more than two thousand Americans were massacred at Pearl Harbor, perhaps anything seemed possible. Great symbols of civilization lay in ruin. Who was to say that Niagara Falls would not suffer a similar fate?

Of course, Niagara Falls did not experience the horrors of war on the homefront. But it certainly prepared for them. On December 10, 1941, it was declared by Rear Admiral Clark H. Woodward that the city of Niagara Falls was a prime target and more of a risk than originally suspected.[83] In fact, he went so far as to point out that "the distance between the Niagara frontier and Europe is shorter than that between Tokyo and Pearl Harbor."[84] Since 1939, American officials had realized that American involvement in the international unrest would be forthcoming, and cities like Niagara Falls had begun planning. No one wanted to be unprepared when the time finally came. Following the Pearl Harbor attacks, Niagara Falls implemented all of its civilian defense measures, and ultimately, the city was safer because of forward-thinking individuals.

Niagara Falls had some unique wartime issues that set the city apart from many of its neighbors. Being a city that shared an international border with Canada made it vulnerable. It was also a major industrial center and power center of the nation. Many of the supplies of war were manufactured in Niagara Falls, making it a possible target for sabotage. Interestingly, because of the city's handling of toxic chemicals for the war effort, many Niagarans made the ultimate sacrifice. The health implications, as well as the environmental implications, are issues that are still relevant today.

There were scrap metal, defense stamp, war bond, victory loan and blood drives. Everyone did their best to contribute to the war effort. Volunteers, the great majority of them women, organized efforts locally to make things easier for our soldiers, airmen and sailors serving abroad. They made bandages, assisted with refugees, organized USO gatherings and sent books to the servicemen and women. They grew Victory Gardens. They bravely suffered through the blackouts, rationing and shortages. Some found creative ways to make life easier.

It was inevitable that a black market would arise from this time of hardship. For Niagara Falls, the illegal transfer of gasoline coupons and other items was carried out in secret operations. One particular young man, who was still in high school, recalled being sent by his father and uncles by train to New York City once a month with an empty suitcase. After arriving in New York City, he would be met by black marketers who filled his empty suitcase with counterfeit ration tickets. He would bring these back to Niagara Falls, where they would be dispersed to various vendors.

"Sometimes it was difficult living with such measures," a source who chooses to remain anonymous remarked.[85]

Gasoline rationing was one of the greater hardships of the war for individuals in East Coast cities like Niagara Falls. "A" stamps were worth three to five gallons of gasoline per week. Only essential driving was permitted, and the national speed limit was dropped to thirty-five miles per hour. As a result of these measures, local gasoline stations were barely able to stay afloat. Those working within the black market sold the counterfeit tickets to the gas vendors, who were then able to use them for customers who requested more gasoline than their rations allowed.

Niagarans tried desperately to make the best of things and to carry on as usual. They attempted to live normal lives as the world seemed to be falling apart. They fell in love and married. Sometimes it seemed almost impossible, but World War II was also a time of great romance. Niagara Falls, referred to by some as the Honeymoon Capital of the World, was inevitably the setting for many a wartime love story.

THE NIAGARA FALLS DEFENSE COUNCIL

The Niagara Falls Defense Council was officially formed on February 21, 1941, by Mayor Ernest W. Mirrington Jr. Representatives of labor, veterans' organizations, utilities and industries were appointed and included the following nine men: Dr. Hector R. Carveth, president of the chamber of commerce; Rob Roy MacLeod, executive vice-president of the Niagara Falls Power Company; Nat P. Anderson, supervisor of service of the Union Carbide Company; William P. Weslar, commander of the John J. Welch Post, American Legion; Walter A. Koske, secretary of the Niagara Falls Federation of Labor; William D. Robbins, city manager; Dr. E.E. Gillick, city health officer; Thomas J. Holohan, superintendent of police; and James H. O'Neil, fire chief. This group of men was endowed with "the power to undertake and promote all things and acts, not inconsistent with city or state to further and promote the state and national defense."[86] They assumed their powers immediately and would continue to do so until the expiration of the act passed by the state legislature that had authorized the establishment of these defense councils.

Right away, the various appointees began establishing groups of volunteers. The first meeting of the volunteer auxiliary police occurred on November 6, 1941. Ninety volunteers met to receive an outline of the course of study that was carefully crafted by the Niagara Falls Defense Council. The course was divided into police administration, traffic control, first aid and bomb squads.[87] Less than one month before the attacks at Pearl Harbor, President Franklin Delano Roosevelt attempted to bolster these civil defense groups across the nation by declaring the week of November 11 through November 16 "Civil Defense Week."

In Niagara Falls, recruiting posts were set up in order to stimulate local residents into action and to prepare for the possibilities of the future. Stations were set up in all sections of the city. In the North End, the stations were set up at Silberberg's and at the North End branch of the Power City Trust Company. In the South End, the stations were set up at Beir Brothers, Amberg and Co. and at the South End branch of Power City Trust Company. In the Pine Avenue area, the station was set up at the Trincanati Electric Co. In LaSalle, the station was set up at Hilt's Pharmacy.

There were openings for 1,800 men and women, including positions within volunteer services such as air raid wardens, auxiliary fire and police, rescue squads, first aid, nursing, ambulance drivers, chemical warfare and explosives. Eventually, at least 2,500 individuals would be required. This

A wartime special police badge belonging to Amy Palumbo. *Courtesy Patricia Palumbo DiNieri.*

Special police, guards at the Carborundum plant. *Courtesy Patricia Palumbo DiNieri.*

would be a volunteer effort with no compensation whatsoever. According to Chairman MacLeod, "This is not a 'pink tea' or 'social event.'"[88] Niagara Falls was preparing for war. Protecting Niagara Falls was not to be taken lightly. The city's industries were considered critical to war production.

> *Most residents of Niagara Falls perhaps do not realize the tremendous importance of this city's industries to defense production. The aluminum, abrasives, alloys, chemicals and other basic materials which are now being made in such tremendous volume in Niagara Falls are in the very front rank of critical materials, without which the defense effort would bog down completely. This narrow strip of land which follows the Niagara River from Lewiston to Woodlawn contains more vital factories than any other strip of similar size in the whole United States. This is no secret, it is as well known to the Axis Powers as it is to the Chamber of Commerce.*[89]

According to Lieutenant Commander Samuel J. Singer, executive assistant to Rear Admiral Clark H. Woodward, in charge of plant production, Office of Civilian Defense, Washington, D.C., "The triangle formed by Buffalo, Niagara, Erie and Pittsburgh is one of the most important defense production areas in the United States."[90] The city of Niagara Falls was listed as number three on the New York state potential target list.[91]

CIVIL AIR PATROL

The only civilian volunteer group performing combat service and privileged to wear the uniform and insignia of the United States Army was the Civil Air Patrol (CAP). An auxiliary of the United States Army Air Forces, CAP included men and women ages sixteen and older with an interest in aviation and military and aeronautical subjects. CAP was organized six days before Pearl Harbor. During the war, CAP was responsible for bombing 82 enemy submarines and ferreting out 173 others, which were then destroyed by army and navy bombers. Fifty-two pilots lost their lives in voluntary service patrolling the coastal waters of the United States and territories during World War II. A plaque commemorates CAP's service during the war at the Niagara Falls Municipal Airport and was dedicated by the Niagara Falls CAP group on December 1, 1956.

Recruitment for the western New York unit began just a few weeks after the Pearl Harbor attacks. On December 18, 1941, a meeting was held at Eagles

Army air forces advertising Civil Air Patrol. *From the Niagara Falls Gazette.*

Hall, between Main Street and Ashland Avenue, in order to begin steps to form a unit in the Niagara region. According to the *Niagara Falls Gazette,* airplanes were "to be furnished by members of the patrol."[92] All pilots, owners of planes and persons interested in flying were urged to join.

The local patrol was designated as Squadron 216-2, "crack squadron in western New York."[93] The squadron meetings were held one evening a week at Niagara Falls High School. CAP courier services operated out of Buffalo and throughout the war assisted the war plants by flying in emergency parts and personnel. One of the more interesting activities of the squadron involved its participation in a mock air raid and exercise for civilian defense forces that was held on Sunday, October 31, 1943. Two thousand civilians participated in this event that involved mainly Falls Street and Buffalo Avenue. CAP was responsible for dropping weighted paper streamers in a simulation of bombs during the exercise.

Stuart C. Welch, group commander of CAP for the Niagara region, said that "the purpose of the Civil Air Patrol is to mobilize and organize civil aviation to make it available to our armed forces in the United States and to preserve civil aviation."[94] Because of the absence of hangar space at the municipal airport at Niagara Falls, it was not possible to have a CAP squad at Niagara Falls.

Several women were also a part of the western New York CAP squadron. Two of them, Dr. Elizabeth Pierce Olmstead and Mary Margaret Woolams, took part in a special demonstration of CAP's capabilities at an air show on September 13, 1942. Woolams had studied primary flights and aerobatics under her husband's instruction at the University of Chicago. She and Jack obtained their degrees, married in six days and headed to Niagara Falls, where Jack had been hired as a test pilot for Bell Aircraft.

A squadron, Niagara Falls Composite Squadron #1, was eventually formed at Niagara Falls under the New York Wing Civil Air Patrol and continues to operate to this day. The squadron meets weekly and is based out of the Niagara Falls Air Reserve Station. Commander Lieutenant Colonel John J. Risio currently leads the group.

THE RED CROSS

The Niagara Falls chapter of the American Red Cross was very active during the war years. Paul S. Brallier served as chairman, along with executive secretary Mrs. Roy Durkin. The War Fund Drive was one of its largest undertakings. The total amounts raised through Red Cross war funds in Niagara Falls were $166,900 (1943), $206,600 (1944) and $195,000 (1945).

The work of the Red Cross was widespread. The majority of the volunteer effort was handled by the women of Niagara Falls. There were numerous committees that kept them busy on the homefront.

The Production Corps, headed by Mrs. Lyman Chandler, oversaw the shipping of over twenty thousand articles of clothing to war zones.

Mrs. Arthur Batts supervised the Knitting Division. Under her leadership, thousands of army and navy garments knitted from wool, which had been furnished by the National Red Cross, were donated to servicemen. This project resulted in over 100,000 hours of volunteer service.

Mrs. John C. McCollum recruited and trained hundreds of women for emergency services with the Nurse's Aides. This group rendered over fifty thousand hours of service. The nurse recruiter, Julia Findlay, contacted every area nurse in order to encourage them to consider military service.

Mrs. Henry P. Kirchner, of First Aid, organized classes immediately following Pearl Harbor. Within eighteen months, 5,145 certificates had been issued in the city of Niagara Falls.

The Motor Corps, also led by Mrs. Henry P. Kirchner, involved maintaining a daily delivery service throughout the war and included an ambulance service for emergencies.

Mrs. E.L. Burhyte, organizer of the Surgical Dressings committee, produced more than one million dressings in five years. Volunteers donated fifty thousand hours of their time at this task.

The Gray Ladies recruited and trained hundreds of volunteer women for service at the two city hospitals and at Fort Niagara. This was led by Mrs. Fred Heil (Memorial Hospital), Mrs. Peter Van Haaren (St. Mary's Hospital), Mrs. Carl H. Richmond (the blood bank) and Mrs. Francis P. Egan (Fort Niagara).

The Home Nursing program was run by Mrs. H. Wesley Clark. This was organized to train at least one woman in each household to care for patients with emergency illnesses.

The Canteen Corps, with Mrs. Charles Moore, served refreshments to guards, servicemen, blood donors and civilian defense workers. It served two hundred dinners at the citywide disaster practice drill held at the Gorge Terminal and aided in hospital kitchens. Its members operated in a mobile canteen donated by the B'nai B'rith. They also held nutrition classes, collected waste fats and canned surplus food.

The Junior Red Cross, with Mrs. George McCartan, worked with the schoolchildren in Niagara Falls. They raised money for war service, furnished books and other articles for servicemen and provided Christmas gifts for patients at the Fort Niagara hospital.

The Home Service Corps, with Mrs. George Comstock and Mrs. Arthur Dunlop, helped to furnish contact between service members and families.

It handled letters, telegrams and personal telephone calls. At times, its members provided emergency financial assistance to those in need.

The Arts and Skills program, with Dr. E.A. Rykenboer, provided training for hospitalized servicemen at Fort Niagara.

Red Cross 1944 war fund. *From* The Tapping Pot, *Electrometallurgical Company*.

The Visiting Nurse Service, with Catherine Martin, involved nearly ten thousand visits to 3,648 cases.

Accident Prevention, with Clifford Seymour, was created to reduce non-industrial accidents in Niagara Falls.

The Life Saving program, with Harold Herkimer, included water safety instruction.

Disaster Preparedness, with Calvin Keller, consisted of traditional Red Cross disaster preparations.[95]

The need for blood donations was very great, and the Red Cross was at the forefront of this essential mission. In England, the blood plasma banks had proven critical in saving civilian lives, and therefore, amassing a large supply in the United States was greatly desired.[96] As a result, the Red Cross began a campaign across the country and in Niagara Falls, thanks to Chairman J. William O'Brien.

Many Niagarans heeded the call and donated their blood for the war effort. By the war's end, fourteen thousand pints of blood had been collected from Niagara Falls and the vicinity.[97] The first members of the Red Cross Two-Gallon Club included a native of Malta and a soldier's wife. Samuel Cutajar, a thirty-eight-year-old war worker, was an operator at the Niagara Alkali plant. He was born on the much-bombed island of Malta but had lived in Niagara Falls since 1920. Jane Ellis, the thirty-five-year-old wife of an officer from Fort Niagara and mother of two young sons, was originally from Ohio. They both had donated more than sixteen pints of blood to the nation's armed forces.

THE AWVS AND THE USO

The American Women's Voluntary Service (AWVS) was a popular national service that was founded in Niagara Falls by Chairman Mrs. Augustus G. Porter in September 1941. Its headquarters were located at 107–11 Main Street, across from the Cataract House hotel. This space was loaned to the organization by the Edson P. Pfohl family. The purpose of this organization was "to encourage women towards mutual aid and also to stimulate enrollment in other local organizations."[98] It had as its slogan, "Unite and Serve."[99] Some of the training done by the AWVS included motor repair work, blackout driving, stretcher and gas mask drill, telegraphy and code practice, map reading, parachute rigging, air raid spotting, advanced first aid and nutrition. Its members also collected war bonds and defense stamps.

Perhaps its most popular effort was the Servicemen's Club. The club, manned by volunteers, offered a comfortable and cheerful place with free appetizing meals for military members. The group also maintained a weekly radio program on the Niagara Falls local station, WHLD.

In October 1943, the AWVS opened the "Blackout Room." This room was open for the general public every day from 10:00 a.m. to 10:00 p.m. and exhibited examples of blackout techniques. It included a test lamp under which residents would place materials to test for light-tight quality. Many different types of blackout curtains were also on display.

By 1944, the AWVS had officially taken over USO activities in the Niagara Falls area. The USO continued to aid in the financing, while the AWVS provided accommodations and personnel for the servicemen's entertainment, as well as refreshments.

WARTIME SALVAGE

Salvage was an important part of the war effort. Various recyclable items were collected in large-scale programs. Perhaps one of Niagara Falls' most symbolic sacrifices included the salvaging of a historic old iron fence that had been erected at 315 Buffalo Avenue during the 1870s by D.J. Townsend. The beautiful fence produced 4,060 pounds of scrap iron. In a stroke of luck, while supervising the removal of the fence, Elton B. Hall, chairman of the Salvage Committee of the Niagara Falls Chapter Red Cross, and Rob Roy McLeod, chairman of the Defense Council, discovered an antique Revolutionary War–era cannon on the premises and added it to the scrap collection. The cannon produced 700 pounds of iron. "In every instance the material collected by the Red Cross, including waste paper, rags, old rubber and scrap metal is placed directly in the hands of a manufacturing firm which can use it. Proceeds from the sale of this material goes into the chapter's emergency fund to be used here."[100]

Another item salvaged was cooking fats. These waste fats were taken to the neighborhood butcher to be handed over as raw material for glycerin used in explosives and gunpowder. L.H. Vanderslice, manager of the Hotel Niagara, was able to provide five hundred pounds per month. His efficient kitchen management was cited as the reason he was able to save this amount of fat. He explained that the homemaker could do the same "in a smaller way."[101] "The more thoroughly you conserve, the more you will save and every spoonful you save helps American boys on the battlefield," he said.[102]

NIAGARA FALLS GAZETTE CARRIERS JOIN THE WAR EFFORT

On December 3, 1941, just four days before the attack at Pearl Harbor, several *Niagara Falls Gazette* carriers officially volunteered as Defense Stamp salesmen.[103] Immediately afterward, the small army of 145 carriers began an ambitious campaign to sell United States Defense Stamps to their customers. The purchase involved a regulation stamp book into which the purchased stamps would be placed. Each book held 187 stamps, and the stamps cost ten

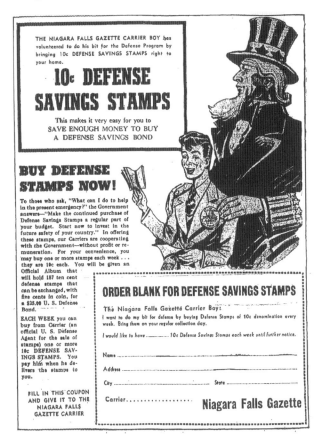

Defense Savings Stamps promoted by the *Niagara Falls Gazette* news carriers. *From* Niagara Falls Gazette.

cents each. Once a book was filled, it could be turned in with an additional five cents to purchase a twenty-five-dollar United States Defense Bond.

The *Gazette* presented each of its carriers who sold 187 stamps with a bronze pin provided by the Treasury Department. One of the young men recognized for his ingenuity in the sale of the stamps was Emerson Dolan of 1865 Linwood Avenue. After receiving the news of the Japanese attack, he decided to go into action. He typed up notices to his sixty customers and asked them to help the nation's defense by buying Defense Stamps from him. He stapled the notice to all of his papers that Monday afternoon. His advertising efforts were successful, as he sold 200 stamps that first week.

By the end of the fourth week of the Defense Stamp sale, it was reported that a total of 59,142 stamps had been sold by *Niagara Falls Gazette* carriers.[104]

BLACKOUTS

Blackouts were taken quite seriously in Niagara Falls. Peter Vendrillo remembers his father-in-law, Nicholas Celenza, an Italian World War I veteran, during the blackouts. Celenza was very proud of his position as an air raid warden and did not hesitate to call to attention those people who did not follow the rules.[105]

Planning the first practice blackout in Niagara Falls was not without issues. The main problem was with the question of the large industrial furnaces. These furnaces normally produced a telltale glow that could be seen for miles. They would not be easy to shut down in such haste. "You can black out our streets, stores and houses but you can't black out our industries," remarked Police Superintendent Thomas Holohan.[106]

The first test was a frontier-wide test. The test would take place at 11:00 p.m. on Friday, December 26, 1941. It was ultimately decided that plant operations would not be interrupted. Under specific orders from the United States War Department, there could be "no cessation of plant operations."[107] Railroad yards also remained lighted, as did other defense-related local activities.

Permission was granted to conduct the simulated blackout on December 20, 1941, and came by telegram from Major General John F. O'Ryan, New York state director of defense. The Niagara Falls Defense Council issued its official notice of a blackout and outlined the details of the exercise and instructions for householders, managers of large premises, pedestrians and

NIAGARA FALLS DEFENSE COUNCIL
AUTHORIZED BY CHAPTER 22, LAWS OF THE STATE OF NEW YORK, 1941

BLACKOUT

CITY OF NIAGARA FALLS

FRIDAY, DECEMBER 26, 1941
11:10 P. M. TO 11:25 P. M.

OFFICIAL   NOTICE

In keeping with the power vested in me by law, I hereby promulgate the following regulations concerning the above blackout:

1. BLACKOUT shall be signalled by sirens, sounding as follows: 1st SIREN (warning signal) sounded for two minutes from 11:00 P. M. to 11:02 P. M. (rising and falling pitch or intermittent blasts). SIX MINUTES is then allowed to blacken ALL LIGHTS in City, and for all people to take their proper places. 2nd SIREN (final warning for blackout) sounded for two minutes from 11:08 P. M. to 11:10 P. M. (rising and falling pitch or intermittent blasts). COMPLETE BLACKOUT FOR FIFTEEN MINUTES (no signals) FROM 11:10 P. M. to 11:25 P. M. ALL CLEAR signal given (two minutes) from 11:25 P. M. to 11:27 P. M. (steady pitch of sirens and steady blast).

2. That all street lights shall be extinguished.

3. That all lights of every kind, both indoor and outdoor, of occupied, unoccupied or unattended premises, except those behind adequate shades which do not permit light to show outside, shall be extinguished when WARNING signal is given and remain extinguished until the ALL CLEAR signal is given.

4. That all lights on outdoor signs of every kind shall be extinguished during the said period.

5. That the provisions of Paragraph 3 shall apply to all premises, including hotels, theatres, stores, restaurants, halls, public buildings, apartment houses, homes, residences and dwellings.

6. That the Supt. of Police of Niagara Falls to which this order applies, may, by permit, grant absolute or conditional exemption from the operation of any of the provisions of the order to vital war industries, hospitals and essential services in this city upon evidence

that operations are involved requiring the use of light which cannot be practicably interrupted or screened. This includes physicians on call.

7. That at the "WARNING" signal all street cars and motor buses shall be stopped and their lights extinguished and all other vehicles including motor cars, motorcycles, horse-drawn vehicles and bicycles, shall be driven to the right-hand curb or right side of the street or highway, stopped and their lights extinguished. All such vehicles shall so remain from the WARNING signal until the ALL CLEAR signal is given.

8. That fire vehicles with lights completely covered with red material, police, ambulance and other emergency service vehicles with lights completely covered with blue material sufficient to eliminate all glare, actually required for police, fire, ambulance and other emergency services shall not be subject to these regulations.

9. That all members of the Niagara Falls Defense Council, Police, Fire and Civilian Defense Forces are empowered to enforce these regulations and to report any violations thereof.

10. That these regulations shall not apply or in any way relate to the naval, military or air services.

11. All plants in the City of Niagara Falls must keep in full production operation throughout this practice blackout. If you are a shift worker, proceed to or from your work as usual but start in time to reach your destination before 11 P. M. Otherwise you will have to conform to section 7.

ERNEST W. MIRRINGTON, Jr.
Mayor of Niagara Falls.

INSTRUCTIONS
(DURING THE BLACKOUT)

TO THE MANAGERS OF LARGE PREMISES:

1. Turn out all exterior lights, including illuminated signs of all types. Turn out or effectively screen all interior lights and screen all skylights. Managers of hotels and apartment houses will be responsible for all blinds being drawn, if light switches are not pulled.
2. See that your staff is fully instructed and acquainted with its duties.
3. Prepare and post up signs to warn the public and staff in your premises.

TO MOTORISTS:

1. Obey the regulations.
2. The streets and highways must be kept clear for the proper and necessary use of Police, Fire, Ambulance and emergency repair vehicles.
3. Pull over to the right-hand curb of the street or roadside and turn off lights and ignition. Avoid parking at street intersections or within twenty-five (25) feet of fire plugs, hospital entrances, or fire hydrants.
4. Avoid congested areas and streets and if possible get into all available parking lots. DO NOT MOVE YOUR CARS AFTER SOUNDING OF THE FINAL WARNING SIGNAL.

TO HOUSEHOLDERS:

1. Stay at home, if possible—it is the safest place in an emergency.
2. Turn out or effectively screen all lights immediately on hearing the WARNING signal.
3. Keep off the streets and highways.
4. Do not light matches or show lights outdoors.
5. Keep your dog under control.
6. Avoid unnecessary use of the telephone.

TO PEDESTRIANS:

1. Remain away from the congested areas.
2. Do not cross streets or highways.
3. At the sounding of the WARNING signal proceed immediately to and remain on the nearest sidewalk or at some place of safety.
4. Do not use matches, lighters or flashlights.

ALL PERSONS ARE REQUIRED TO COOPERATE AND FOLLOW THE ABOVE INSTRUCTIONS, ISSUED BY THE NIAGARA FALLS DEFENSE COUNCIL AND FIRE DEPARTMENTS.

Niagara Falls, N. Y.,
December 25, 1941.

THOMAS J. HOLORAN,
Superintendent of Police.

Failure to comply with above regulations will be prosecuted to the full extent of the law.

Blackout notice. *From* Niagara Falls Gazette.

motorists. All persons were required to cooperate and were responsible for understanding the rules.

On the night of December 26, 1941, Niagara Falls and many other cities throughout the region went black. One of the world's most lighted cities became a ghost town at the first warning. Christmas tree lights, automobile headlights, houses, stores and businesses were immediately blotted. The air raid wardens successfully manned their posts and herded late stragglers into the safety of public buildings. Nearly one million people took part in the blackout on the Niagara frontier. One arrest was made in Niagara Falls concerning an individual who failed to pull his car to the curb and extinguish his lights. Some of the area plants (not involved with war production) took part in the blackout. The Niagara Falls Power Company extinguished all but necessary lights. The Shredded Wheat Company participated in a total blackout and even turned its building over to civilian defense workers.

In Niagara Falls, over 1,700 civil defense individuals were on duty. Some spotters situated themselves on rooftops from Niagara University to LaSalle. The list of violators would be turned in to police headquarters the following day. One of the most critical things noted during the exercise was the reflection of lights from Canada (which did not participate) against some of the buildings on the American side. The moon also proved problematic, as the light reflected on the wet city streets, as well as on the tops of automobiles.

Niagara Falls civil defense officials and city officials watched the blackout proceedings from atop the Hotel Niagara. They were pleased with the results. Rob Roy McLeod, head of the Civil Defense Council, said that from his vantage point it was "remarkable to watch the speed with which the people of the city complied with the blackout regulations."[108] He went on to state that "we had made our preparations and we have had our test. The success of the latter is adequate proof that the plans that we made and the trouble that we went to were not in vain."[109]

By 1943, new blackout rules had been incorporated in Niagara Falls. Blackouts could occur at any time, and the residents needed to be ready for them. The general rule was that when the first signal sounded, residents needed to put up blackout curtains and extinguish all lights. The next step was to turn on the radio and tune into any of the local Buffalo stations. No matter what was happening outside the home, the lights needed to be kept off until the all-clear was given on the radio.

TO ILLUMINATE OR NOT TO ILLUMINATE

There were certain wartime situations that were specific to Niagara Falls. Of course, other major industrial cities had the issue of the factory furnaces during the blackouts, as well. One very specific local concern dealt with the illumination of Niagara Falls.

Niagara Falls has been gloriously lit during the nighttime hours, on and off, for over 150 years. Part of the Niagara experience is to observe the great cataract at nighttime. Various types of illumination were utilized through the centuries. At one time, Bengal lights were used along the banks

The American falls illuminated, 1940s. *Author's collection.*

and below the American falls. Illumination with electricity first occurred in 1879. By 1892, searchlights had been added, with lamps of 2,000 candlepower placed in the gorge at a distance of 250 feet. There was special lighting for the Pan-American Exposition in 1901. By 1907, the General Electric Company had harnessed a greater amount of power, with 1,115,000,000-candlepower lights. In 1925, the Falls Illumination Board was created to set up, finance, operate and maintain a new permanent lighting system. At this time, twenty-four carbon searchlights were installed, along with lighting at 1,320,000,000 candlepower. Niagara Falls has been illuminated most nights since 1925.

During the fall of 1941, it was decided that illumination of the falls was to be abandoned for the duration of the war. The lights were dismantled and put away. It was believed that it was a way to conserve power. They did go on again for Memorial Day in 1942, but they had been darkened again by Labor Day. Finally, after much debate, the Ontario Hydro Company, the Canadian government, the United States government and the Niagara Falls Illumination Board agreed that the small amount of power used for the lighting would not interfere with war industries. An agreement was reached that the lights could go back on but would be "cancelled for any real or practice blackouts."[110] They would be on for two and a half hours nightly until September 15 and then would shut down for the winter season.

It was cause for celebration when the lights were switched back on at Niagara Falls on Sunday, October 22, 1944. A formal ceremony was held at Niagara Falls. Twenty-four spotlights and 1,296,000,000 candlepower of light were displayed. Mayor George R. Inglish of Niagara Falls, Ontario, and Councilman Wilbur F. Connell of Niagara Falls, New York, did the formal button pressing. "First there was a solid barrage of light. Then from the cases where they had been placed on September 10, 1942, were taken the huge colored sheets by which could be simulated the rainbow effect on the falls."[111]

After two years of darkness, there was light. "The renewal reflects confidence of officials in the security of the American continent from attack." Niagara Falls, this great symbol of America's strength, was blazing, once again, on even the blackest of nights.

WAR GAS FACTS AND CHEMICAL EXPOSURE

During the war, the head of the Chemical Protection division of the Civilian Defense Council, Dr. Wilmer H. Koch, published a series of articles in the *Niagara Falls Gazette* to educate Niagarans about the dangers of exposure to dangerous chemicals. Contamination was always a possibility. The threat of industrial sabotage was a serious concern.

There was also a very real concern regarding the release of injurious gases from the plants. Gases from the Chemical Warfare plant, located on Buffalo Avenue, adjacent to the Echota residential area, were causing quite a stir in 1942 and 1943. Noxious gases were menacing the neighborhood to such an extent that in August 1943, sixty-eight petitioners demanded assistance from the City of Niagara Falls. While the signers professed to be "loyal Americans," they did not see why they should have to live under such terrible health conditions.[112] It was stated that "every bit of green vegetation in the locality" had been destroyed by the gases.[113] Parks Superintendent E.R. Werner acknowledged that 160 city trees had been destroyed by the fumes.[114] City Health Officer Dr. E.E. Gillick filed the reports and replied that "while the condition is definitely annoying it is not dangerous to health or life."[115] Officials had been hopeful when this all began, in May 1942, that perhaps shifts in the winds would save the trees, but they were incorrect.

In an industrial city such as Niagara Falls, residents dealt with the threat of chemicals on a daily basis. A majority of the residents were employed by the

Plant police and hospital staff demonstrate gas masks as part of evacuation training. *From The Tapping Pot, Electrometallurgical Company.*

plants that produced many tons of several different chemicals and war gases and were exposed to potential danger on a daily basis. Dr. Koch was fearful that the gases manufactured here could be subject to sabotage. This was not only a danger to the plants and areas nearby. These hazardous materials were shipped out of the city on a daily basis over every railroad crossing. "The major concern of every citizen should be gas," he stated in February 1943.[116]

The main gases that were present in the city of Niagara Falls that were of greatest concern included chlorine, phosgene, chloropicrin, mustard gas, Lewisite, chloroacetophenone, Adamsite and phosphorus. They could be recognized by odor and by their reaction in the nose or eyes. In his write-ups, Dr. Koch explained how citizens could learn that an exposure was occurring and what to do. He instructed his readers to do several things. First of all, gas masks were vital to survival. In fact, Dr. Koch was quite irritated that a city such as Niagara Falls was not issued adequate gas masks. Without a gas mask, the only other hope for survival was refuge in a gas-proof shelter. He gave detailed instructions for building such a structure. If both of these measures were unavailable, it was critical to reach higher ground, as gases are heavier than air and tend to dissipate at higher levels.

Under measures supported by the Niagara Falls Civilian Defense Council, special squads were organized in Niagara Falls and members were trained in decontamination. Techniques were learned for cleaning streets, buildings and transportation equipment. Niagara was preparing for the unthinkable but at the same time actually suffering the effects of the noxious gases through wartime work in the plants or through living and breathing in a community inundated with deadly but unseen chemicals. This legacy of chemical exposure would carry into the future and, unfortunately, become a dismal reality for the city of Niagara Falls.

A WARTIME WEDDING

Jean Fortuna and Henry Borgatti had the misfortune of falling in love in the midst of a world war. Jean, a war worker for Bell Aircraft in Niagara Falls, met Henry in Welland, Ontario, Canada, just across the border. Henry lived in the Cordage apartments, which were the living quarters for the workers of the Plymouth Cordage Company. Both Jean and Henry were the children of Italian immigrants. Shortly after Canada's entry into World War II, in 1939, Henry and his brother, Armando, joined the service. Armando joined the army, and Henry joined the Royal Canadian Air Force (RCAF). Their mother, Louisa Borgatti, was not happy that they had joined. She disliked the fact that she would have two sons in the war.

Jean never really thought the wedding would take place. "I just wondered if maybe we weren't meant to be together," she said.[117] Everything seemed to go wrong from the beginning. They were supposed to be married in September. Because of the war and the fact that Henry's leave was continually cancelled, their wedding date was postponed three times. The invitations had to be redone each time. Finally, a date was set for December 21, 1944. But there was even trouble with this date, as it would take place during the Roman Catholic season of Advent. Traditionally, weddings were not allowed during Advent. Father Carey of St. Joseph's Church on Pine Avenue arranged for special dispensation from the bishop in Buffalo in order for the wedding to take place.

It had not been easy to find a dress, either. Jean and her mother, Clementina Fortuna, found that there were no adequate gowns available in the city of Niagara Falls. Because of the lack of silk and other materials, there were not many choices for the wartime bride. Most of the gowns were old and not at all stylish.

Clementina suggested they go to Buffalo, where there were more selections. They took a bus, and when they arrived at Berger's Department Store, the saleswomen apologized after informing the women that, like

Niagara Falls, they really only had a few picked-over dresses. But just as Mrs. Fortuna and her daughter were about to leave, one of the saleswomen stopped them. A new shipment had just arrived. It was only one bridal gown, but at least it could be a possibility. When they opened the box, Jean knew at once that this was the dress she would wear when she married Henry Borgatti. "It was a miracle," she said.[118]

Still other troubles followed the couple. Due to strict rationing practices, there was not enough sugar for the shower cakes. The women canvassed the neighborhoods for donations. Weddings and other events often required cakes and baked desserts, and it was common practice for neighbors, friends and family to pool supplies.

The day of the wedding was cold and wintry. The women's dresses were inappropriate for the season due to the fact that the wedding had originally been planned for the fall. The flowers delivered were the wrong order. Jean had ordered colonial bouquets, and instead she was delivered (late) modern cascades. The dirty, gasoline-soaked snow at the curbside stained her gown as she exited the automobile. Her grandmother Adelina Ventresca was slightly injured in an automobile accident during the short drive from their home to the church. Jean said that suddenly everything seemed as if it would be all right when her father, Frank Fortuna, walked her down the aisle at St. Joseph's Church. Henry was there, and the wedding was actually taking place. Love had triumphed after all.

What Jean did not know was that in order to marry her, Henry had been forced to go absent without leave (AWOL) from his unit with the RCAF. He had confided in his chaplain how desperate he was to marry Jean and told him that he knew he would be breaking the law. He would only be doing this for love, he told him. He just did not want to lose his chance of marrying Jean Fortuna.

Jean and Henry honeymooned in Rochester, New York. They boarded the New York Central Railroad at Third Street and traveled east. They spent one night in a hotel. Jean's friend Clementine Irene, a fellow war worker at Bell Aircraft who worked under her, invited them to her home in Rochester for a Christmas celebration. Clementine's husband was away serving with the army in France. Through the war, she lived in Niagara Falls with her parents, who babysat her young son while she worked, but she kept her home in Rochester as well.

By Sunday, the couple had returned to Niagara Falls. Jean had to get back to work, and Henry did not know what to expect when he returned to his post. Upon arriving at the bridge to Canada, the military police were waiting for him. He was charged with being AWOL and leaving the country.

The wartime wedding of Henry Borgatti and Jean Fortuna, December 21, 1944. *From left to right*: Joseph Fortuna, Henry Borgatti, Jean Fortuna, Clementina Fortuna and Frank Fortuna. *Courtesy Jean Borgatti.*

But thanks to the sympathetic chaplain, his punishment was not too severe. He was made to work KP duty for a month.

Married life was not quite normal during the war. Jean went back to her parents and her war work. Henry was transferred to Toronto and then to Centralia and finally across the country to Vancouver. He stayed there awaiting final orders to India. Henry was a wireless radio instructor for the RCAF. They lived separately like this until the war ended and they were allowed to be together again.

LIFE IN NIAGARA FALLS

Marie (Gorrow) Myers remembers when she first heard about Pearl Harbor. She was living on Youngstown-Lockport Road at the time. She was newly married, and she and her husband were at a local hangout with friends on

Mother and son, Blanche and Edward Gorrow. Blanche is wearing her Bell Aircraft coveralls. *Courtesy Marie (Gorrow) Myers.*

Creek Road when the news came to them. Everyone was talking about it. Pearl Harbor had been attacked.

She spent most of the war years struggling as a young wife and mother. Marie, her husband and their infant child moved to an upstairs apartment on Ontario Avenue in Niagara Falls. There was a housing shortage, and good places were hard to find. This apartment was not an ideal place to raise a family, but there really were no other options. Initially the downstairs apartment was a furniture storage unit. Soon after they moved in, it became a noisy bar. Sometimes there was so much carousing downstairs that the furniture upstairs shook.

Marie worked as a riveter for Bell Aircraft. When she and her husband discovered they were expecting another child, she gave up her job. Her mother, Blanche Gorrow, who had been babysitting for her, replaced her at Bell Aircraft.

Like other wartime women in Niagara Falls, Marie salvaged her old pots and pans. She also donated many books to the Victory Book drives. She reminisced about the blackouts and the rationing. Her husband had been a truck driver, and according to Marie, "he hauled bombs." She was not sure where these bombs came from or where he took them. She only knew that he had a dangerous job.

Four of Marie's brothers were in the service. They all made it back. One of her brothers was in Japan. He told her that if there ever was another war, he would refuse to go. He had experienced Japanese kamikaze pilot attacks, and they left a lasting impression. Many of the boys she graduated with did not come home. Two of Marie's cousins died in the war. One of her fondest memories was reading Ernie Pyle's columns in the *Niagara Falls Gazette*. "Even he was killed," she told me.

When the war ended, all of Niagara Falls celebrated. The streetcars were free that day, and Marie and her husband spent the day hopping on and off and socializing all over town.

"I was young," she said, "and even while there was a war on, it was a very exciting time."[119]

Throughout the years, Marie has written poetry about many things, including life during World War II. The following is one of her poems about the war.

CHEERIO JOHNNY

Thru the murky fog of London morn
There came a measured tread
They were leaving for the battle
The young dough boys marched ahead.

The rosy cheeked young maiden
Who stood waiting with the rest
To cheer the boys to victory
Clutched icy fingers to her breast.

A gasp, a sob tore from her lips
No doubt left in her mind
There in front with his captain
Her sweetheart led the line.

As he passed along beside her
Pleading arms she stretched his way
His eyes begged her forgiveness
Their love would be again someday.

Oh, cheerio my Johnny
I will always wait for you.
Cheerio, my Johnny
I will forever more be true.

The years went on, the war long won
Ours was the victory.
The doughboys left the shores of England
Home to their land across the sea.

Like a rose without the summer's sun
She faded day by day
Never hearing from her soldier
They could hear the maiden say:

Cheerio, my Johnny
I will always wait for you.
Cheerio, my Johnny
I'll forever more be true.

The months, the years, see children play
Around the cottage door
Where sits a hag with straggled tress
They heed her voice no more.

The muttered tone goes on and on
A never changed refrain
They seldom stop to hear or stare
As she cries again, again.

Oh, cheerio my Johnny
I will always wait for you.
Cheerio, my Johnny
I will forever more be true.[120]

Chapter 6

BELL AIRCRAFT AND CAMP BELL

T he story of Niagara Falls in World War II could not be told without a review of the history of Bell Aircraft and Camp Bell. Not only did the wartime plant manufacture planes such as the P-39 Airacobra, a fighter plane that generated "the highest number of individual kills recorded by a U.S. produced fighter aircraft during the war,"[121] and the P-63 Kingcobra, but tens of thousands of Niagarans, including many women, spent the war years on the assembly lines in order to contribute to an Allied victory.

Although Camp Bell (née Cataract) came to be through a "hasty uncertain conception," it quickly grew into a world-class training center for fighter plane specialists.[122] Located near the Niagara Falls airport, it was a joint operation between Bell Aircraft and the army. The Army Air Forces Technical Training Command (AAFTTC) graduated 7,432 aircraft maintenance men between 1942 and 1944 at the center.

Along with the aircraft, the mechanics and the war production workers, there were also a group of pilots stationed in Niagara Falls during the war. They operated under a wing of the Bell Aircraft Flight Department and were employed in the most dangerous business of testing the aircraft. Not unlike the daredevils of Niagara's past, they came to conquer fear itself. There were great victories, but there were also great tragedies.

THE SPIRIT OF THIS PLACE

The news could not have been better: Niagara Falls was set to become the site of Bell Aircraft's newest venture. Betty Harries, *Niagara Falls Gazette* reporter, was caught in an air of excitement as she ventured into the "sanctum of President Bell himself."[123] She found the Buffalo office of Lawrence Bell, president of Bell Aircraft, located at 2050 Elmwood Avenue, "guarded and busy."[124] Laid out before her were enlarged air views of the Niagara Falls Municipal Airport, as well as architects' drawings of the building that would go up in Niagara Falls. Bell was certain that the plant would be beneficial for both Niagara Falls and his company. It seemed like the perfect match. He had been considering the airport for a possible site for his new plant for some time. "Its approaches are superb and there are no obstructions on the field. I like the spirit of this place," he told her.[125]

The Niagara Falls Municipal Airport formally opened on June 13, 1929. It became "one of the country's most modern small airports."[126] The airport was first used by Skyview Airlines, which erected an administration

Bell Aircraft plant in Niagara Falls, 1940s. *Courtesy Niagara Aerospace Museum and Archives.*

The flight line at Bell Aircraft, 1940s. *Courtesy Niagara Aerospace Museum and Archives.*

building and hangar. In its early days, it was considered "small, unlighted" and containing "inadequate runways made of slag."[127] It was improved by the Works Progress Administration (WPA) during the Depression years. Its runways were macadamized and extended to 2,500 feet in length. Other WPA projects, with the assistance of the Civil Aeronautics Authority, contributed to additional funds for the construction of an east–west runway 4,000 feet long and 200 feet wide. This lengthening proved adequate for all the war traffic at the field. Its runways could handle the largest and most heavily loaded planes. In fact, during the war years, the airport was the site of the take-off and landing of about one hundred planes per day.

On December 15, 1941, just about a week following the Japanese attack at Pearl Harbor, the Bell Aircraft Corporation, upon the insistence of the War Department of the United States, took control of the hangar at the Niagara Falls Municipal Airport. The manager of the airport, Richard C. Bonhurst, immediately reported that the use of the field for private flying purposes was limited to those connected with government training programs.[128] The handing over of the field to the plant allowed for an expansion of Bell Aircraft's Niagara Falls facilities and precipitated an immediate buildup in the manufacturing of military aircraft.

LAWRENCE D. BELL

Lawrence D. Bell, or "Larry," as he was familiarly known, was born on April 5, 1894, in Mentone, Indiana. His interest in flying had been imparted to him by his older brother, Grover E. Bell. Grover was a well-known flyer, and Larry learned about airplanes while working as his mechanic. He soon learned to fly himself. Following his brother's death during an exhibition flight on July 4, 1913, Larry considered giving up aviation. That was short-lived, however, for at just about twenty years of age, he was hired by the Glenn L. Martin Company, an American aircraft manufacturer. By 1928, he was working as

a sales manager with Reuben H. Fleet's Consolidated Aircraft in Buffalo, New York. Within a year, he was vice-president and general manager. On July 10, 1935, one year after Consolidated Aircraft transferred to the West Coast, Bell returned to Buffalo and opened the Bell Aircraft Corporation on the site of Consolidated Aircraft. In order to raise the needed capital for this venture, he "trudged through the streets ringing doorbells [of potential investors] in search of the $170,000 needed to begin work."[129] In less than a year's time, he had raised enough money to start up and soon after became head of one of the nation's greatest manufacturing companies.

Larry Bell. *Courtesy Niagara Aerospace Museum and Archives.*

THE NIAGARA FALLS PLANT

Operations officially began at the Niagara Falls site of the Bell Aircraft Corporation on May 19, 1941. The $1,250,000 plant was first agreed upon at a Niagara Falls City Council meeting held on September 27, 1940, in which the contract was drawn up allowing Bell to utilize the Niagara Falls Municipal Airport. By August 1941, the United States government had approved an $8,456,175 project that would expand the factory from 240,000 to 950,000 square feet. It would include more office space, an engineering building, a hangar, an employment office, a shipping building and other space necessary for the fabrication of the Bell P-39 Airacobra parts. Niagara Falls would become one of the primary production sites for the P-39 Airacobra, as well as the P-63 Kingcobra.

This sixty-three-acre site adjacent to the Niagara Falls airport included a provision for 240,000 square feet of additional floor space. The original structure completed in 1941 measured 600 feet by 400 feet and was divided

Bell Aircraft workers. *Courtesy Niagara Aerospace Museum and Archives.*

into three bays. The six power-driven assembly lines were located in the center bay, which was 200 feet wide, with columns 100 feet apart for 400 feet of its length. The north and south bays were used for fabrication of sub-assemblies not completed at the Buffalo location.

One of the most important steps taken at the Niagara Falls plant was to dramatically simplify construction techniques and move toward a mass production goal. Several machines aided in this transition. The mechanical assembly line allowed for constant motion through two lines by means of

Bell victory shift. *From* Niagara Falls Gazette.

endless chains that were sunk into the floor. They moved at the rate of a fraction of an inch a minute. Several other lines were also added to speed up production. High-speed electric drills and routers were in place and mounted on double tables, which moved along a center-line track. Operators stood to one side and traced template parts and spotted rivet holes. Across the table were sheets of aluminum alloys piled up to twelve feet high. There were mechanical paint-dipping machines on an endless chain four hundred feet long with two dip tanks and infrared ray drying lamps. At least 1,500 pieces could be given a primary protective coat of yellow chrome and a second dipping of olive green per hour.

In addition to these special-purpose machines, there was a mechanical overhead conveyor to carry materials to stations. Metal baskets capable of carrying one hundred pounds of parts or materials would be used on the conveyors, which moved ahead at forty feet per minute. Hydraulic presses also used at Bell included drop hammer batteries, stamping machines, spot welders and gang riveters.

The plant at Niagara Falls was a model of productivity. After the war, Larry Bell mentioned that what he generated in Niagara Falls was actually a re-creation of one of the ultra-modern facilities he had visited in Germany during the 1930s: "Bell Aircraft's new plant was a duplicate of that factory—copied right out, because it was the most modern thing I had ever seen."[130]

By 1944, the Niagara Frontier division of the Bell Aircraft Corporation (including Buffalo and Niagara Falls) had manufactured 12,200 fighter planes.[131] The Bell plant at Niagara Falls was acclaimed for its efficiency. Developments such as the steps taken toward mass production resulted in a reduction of man hours and greatly increased the total number of planes produced.

THE AIRCRAFT

When Larry Bell first conceived of the notion of manufacturing planes, he and his designers decided that the plane they would initially produce would be unique. The result was the Airacuda, which incorporated their conviction that the main purpose of a pursuit plane was "to hurtle the greatest volume possible of destructive fire power through the skies as speedily as possible."[132] Completed in 1937, the Airacuda was a multi-seater, two-engine pusher propeller ship. Only fourteen were made, and they were purchased by the United States Army for training.

The assembly line at Bell Aircraft. *Courtesy Niagara Aerospace Museum and Archives.*

The Airacuda eventually gave way to the much-celebrated P-39 Airacobra. This design was much smaller and built for speed and firepower. Its initial test flight was in May 1939. On September 13, 1939, the army awarded Bell its first contract for thirty P-39 Airacobras. This order grew to hundreds and then to thousands.

The P-39 Airacobra was the only one of its kind and carried a thirty-seven-millimeter cannon that fired through the hub of the propeller. Its accuracy and destructive power were praised. The P-39 Airacobra also included .30- and .50-caliber machine guns. The two larger guns fired through the propeller, and the other fired through the wings. The Allison Prestone cooled engine located behind the pilot was an innovation in airplane construction. Bulletproof glass and armor plates were also added features of this plane. A tricycle landing gear permitted pilots to land on unpaved roads or in muddy fields. Most of the P-39 Airacobras assembled at the Niagara Falls plant were delivered to the United States Army. The Buffalo plant provided the same for Great Britain. Mass production began in the summer of 1941 and continued until the last of the planes on the assembly lines were completed in July 1944. They were made obsolete because of their altitude limitations. Even as the P-39 Airacobras were designed as interceptors, they were also used as escort fighters, dive bombers, skip bombers, ground strafers, observers and over-the-water rescue ships.

The first rave notice for the P-39 Airacobra came from Associated Press combat reporter J. Wes Gallagher:

> The U.S. built Airacobra has been stamped the best pursuit plane in the air by pilots of the 1ˢᵗ RAF Squadron using this American-made fighter plane, just back from two days of forays across the Channel. The Airacobras shot up a ship in the Channel, riddled harbor installations with cannon and machine gun fire and returned to their bases without encountering German fighters.[133]

Niagarans were quite proud of these locally assembled Airacobras. On September 11, 1943, the merchants committee of Falls Street arranged to display a P-39 Airacobra in front of the Strand and Cataract Theatres as a special prop to help drive sales of bonds in the third war loan drive. Although the planes were a familiar sight in the skies over Niagara, not many people had the opportunity to see one up close. As a special bonus, alongside the booth that sold the war bonds and the plane was a sign that read, "We'll drop this book on Hitler's lap!" People who purchased war bonds were invited to sign a book that would be dropped over a German target.[134]

The city's schoolchildren also found some interest in Bell's top plane. They raised over $66,000 through the sale of war stamps to purchase an Airacobra that was to be sent to Brigadier General Harold H. George, a former student from Niagara Falls High School who was serving as an aide to General Douglass MacArthur and his chief air corps officer. They chose to do this as a token of respect and admiration for his exploits in the Philippine Islands. Unfortunately, General George was killed on April 27, 1942, in an airplane crash. Upon hearing of his death, Mayor Ernest W. Mirrington Jr. ordered all flags in Niagara Falls to be flown at half-staff in honor of Niagara Falls' "No. 1 Soldier."[135] The city was heartbroken. As a result, the students and faculty raised more money—enough to purchase a Curtis bomber. Upon the suggestion of a Seventeenth Street School student, fourth grader Amel Kinan of 1513 Pierce Avenue, the new bomber would be named for and dedicated to General George. The superintendent of schools, James F. Taylor, couldn't agree more.

Brigadier General Harold Huston George. *From the U.S. War Department.*

In 1941, in an attempt to correct deficiencies in the P-39 Airacobra design, Bell created the P-63 Kingcobra. These were also manufactured at Niagara Falls. Ultimately, the P-63 Kingcobra found more success abroad than at home due to the fact that it exhibited a poor high-altitude performance. It worked best "under the radar" and was used primarily by the USSR in low-altitude attacks.

The P-63 Kingcobra featured a rear-mounted engine that turned a three-bladed propeller system by way of a shaft that ran under the cockpit floor. A thirty-seven-millimeter Oldsmobile M4 cannon was fitted into the engine cowl and used for firing through the propeller blades. Four .30-caliber machine guns were supplied on the wings. Another feature was the utilization of the laminar-flow wing, which used symmetrical air foil to minimize drag. The P-63 Kingcobra was the only United States fighter plane to begin production and go into combat after the start of World War II.

These planes were a part of the Lend-Lease program and were often ferried to the USSR from the plants at Niagara Falls and Buffalo by female pilots. There were two main routes by which the planes reached their destination. One route began in Niagara Falls; went on to Selfridge Field, Michigan, and Truax Field, Wisconsin; and, upon being picked up by a female Russian pilot, would then be flown via Anchorage to the USSR. Another route that also began in Niagara Falls went through Great Falls, Montana, to Fairbanks, Alaska, and then on to Siberia. It has been estimated that around 2,400 P-63 Kingcobras were sent to the USSR in this manner.

P-39s over Niagara Falls. *Courtesy Niagara Aerospace Museum and Archives.*

THE *MISS LEND-LEASE*

Perhaps one of the most haunting exhibits at the Niagara Aerospace Museum, located at 9900 Porter Road at the Niagara Falls International Airport, is the *Miss Lend-Lease*. It is so real that the observer almost feels as if he or she is not in a museum at all but on the edge of Lake Mart-Yavr, near the city of Murmansk in Russia. The badly beaten plane has not been restored but rather conserved in an attempt to relay more of a realistic connection to history. The intent was "to show how it landed on the ice at the end of its flying trail."[136]

It was actually quite remarkable how it all unfolded and how a P-39 Airacobra made it back home to its final resting place in western New York. It all began in July 2004, when an old fisherman thought he saw something in the lake. Soon after reporting his finding, a warbird recovery team from Great Britain searched the lake and ultimately retrieved one of the "most remarkable artifacts ever collected."[137] After it was released from its

101

watery grave on August 19, 2004, the *Miss Lend-Lease* was found to contain the remains of twenty-two-year-old Soviet combat pilot Lieutenant Ivan Ivanovich Baranovsky. After sixty years, he was finally given a hero's burial. There were also other items found within the plane. There were small cans of food stashed inside ammunition bays labeled "Made in USA." The flight records and log book were also extracted. With all this information, it was possible to determine a great deal about the ill-fated *Miss Lend-Lease*.

The *Miss Lend-Lease* went down during a ferrying mission on November 19, 1944. However, that is not the end of its story, for the records that were found inside the plane traced the passage of P-39Q no. 44-2911 from Buffalo, through a string of United States air bases, to Alaska and then on to the USSR. It was one of many Lend-Lease P-39 Airacobras that were sent to the USSR—"only this is the only one that made it back."[138] Remarkably, the signatures of two of the women who worked on the plane, Helen Rose and Eleanor Barbaritano, were found still intact on the instrument panel.

In 2009, the Niagara Aerospace Museum purchased the *Miss Lend-Lease* for $400,000 and brought it "home" to western New York. The exhibit is a celebration of the contributions of so many western New Yorkers during the war. According to Hugh Neeson, a former vice-president and general manager of Bell, as well as the development director for the Niagara Aerospace Museum, the *Miss Lend-Lease* is "a real living tribute to the

The *Miss Lend-Lease* at the Niagara Aerospace Museum. *Courtesy Tim Baxter.*

tremendous effort put out by western New York in World War II as part of the overall nation and the Allies' effort to marshal all forces to ultimately produce 30,000 aircraft for America and its allies. That's 10% of aircraft production in the United States."[139]

RISKY BUSINESS

Daredevils will always find their way to Niagara Falls. Over the years, the river has summoned many risk-taking men and women. In 1901, Annie Edson Taylor was the first woman to survive a trip over the Horseshoe Falls in a barrel. Others had great courage as well, but they were not as lucky. During the war years, Bell Aircraft found it necessary to demonstrate that its airplanes met all contractual specifications, including flight performance. A flight test program was developed in order to fulfill these demands. As a result, a crew of test pilots was enlisted. There was a degree of hazard associated with this position, and some of the men were lost. But there was a war going on, and everyone had a job to do. Those qualified and willing took on the challenge.

The Bell Aircraft Flight Department employed about thirty-seven test pilots.[140] Some of the main test pilots who worked with the P-39 Airacobras and other aircraft during the war included Frank H. Kelley Jr., Robert M. Stanley, Mark Heaney, Arthur W. Nelson and Jack Woolams.

Jack Woolams had accomplished a great deal for a man who had not yet reached thirty years of age. He was nationally known for his flying prowess. He joined the team at Bell Aircraft in June 1941. He worked mainly with the experimental research division and in 1944 was promoted to chief test pilot.

Woolams held many world records. On October 2, 1942, he flew the first transcontinental flight from March Field, California, to Bolling Field, Washington, D.C., in a fighter plane. In 1943, he also set a new altitude record of 47,600 feet. He was to be the first pilot to fly Bell's XS-1, and it was presumed that in this plane he would "crash the mysterious barrier of speed faster than sound."[141] The XS-1, an experimental plane built for the army air forces, was made to travel up to 1,500 miles per hour. It was the first plane ever constructed to fly faster than the speed of sound. According to the air force, it was considered "the most important mission an airman has undertaken since man's first flight."[142] The sound barrier was eventually

Jack Woolams, chief test pilot. *Courtesy Niagara Aerospace Museum and Archives.*

broken in the Bell XS-1, but Woolams was not flying it. Instead, a pilot named Charles "Chuck" Yaeger had the honors.

Woolams professed to have no fear of flying. Brushes with death were a common feature of his job. He had to bail out of planes a number of times. Ultimately, Woolams dreamed that he would one day "fly a spaceship between the vast unknown regions between the planets."[143]

Unfortunately, that was not to be, for on a beautiful summer's day in August 1946, his life was lost over Lake Ontario. He was testing a souped-up P-39 Airacobra that he had planned on flying for the upcoming National Air Races in Cleveland, Ohio. Instead, something went terribly wrong, and he crashed into the water. He was only twenty-nine years old.

A Portrait of a Female Wartime Worker

Jean Fortuna was only in tenth grade when she began working at Bell Aircraft. Due to the fact that she had *accidentally* left her birth certificate at home when she went to the employment office at the new Bell factory, she was hired as an adult worker. Lina Trincanati, a neighbor, already worked at Bell and had suggested that Jean apply, as the company was desperately seeking workers. "I just wanted to do something for the war effort," Jean said.[144]

She was hired for the second shift, which ran from 4:30 p.m. to 1:00 a.m. She had a daily routine that seemed to make things work, although at times it was difficult balancing school and her work at Bell Aircraft. But Jean did not want to give up on either. She had dreams of one day going to college and becoming a nurse—and these dreams eventually did come true about twenty years later. She also wanted to do whatever she could to help the Allies win the war.

Clementina Fortuna, Jean's mother, tried to make things easier for her daughter by making sure her uniform (a navy blue one-piece jumper with the Bell insignia and a head wrap) was all set. She would also prepare an afterschool snack of either soup or Jell-O. Jean would sometimes pack a lunch or eat soup or a sandwich on her break at Bell's cafeteria. Clementina also contributed to the war effort in Niagara Falls. She had been a chef at the famed Cataract House, and when the army moved its men, who had initially been set up in a makeshift training camp at the hotel, to the newly built Camp Bell (by the Niagara Falls Municipal Airport), she went along with the troops.

Jean worked the assembly line for some time until the foreman realized that perhaps she was a bit too young to be working the drills. They met with Evelyn Ishman, personnel director, and it was decided that Jean would be transferred to the stockroom. In this position, during downtime, she would be able to do some homework.

Even at ninety-one years of age, Jean remembers her wartime work quite well. She worked on top of the catwalk. When the foreman would call up to a station and ask for a kit, Jean would search for the kit along the shelves in the storeroom and then attach it to a basket that would be lowered to the floor below. Each kit was for a particular plane. When she worked in this department, she did not have to wear a uniform anymore. Jean was promoted on the day she graduated from Niagara Falls High School. She was appointed leadwoman of #2 conveyor on June 21, 1943.

At shift changes, thousands of people entered and exited the plant. There was a lot of rushing around. There were guards at every door. The workers

Camp Bell cooking staff. *From left*: Clementina Fortuna; Ethel Mt. Pleasant Zomont; and the head chef, Jack (last name unknown). The last two men have not been identified. *Courtesy Jean Borgatti.*

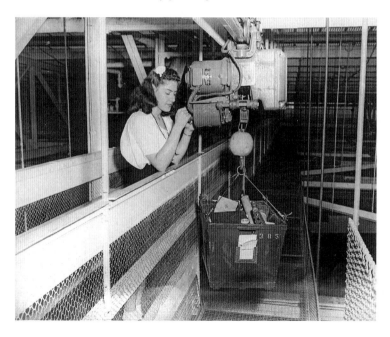

Jean Fortuna, Bell Aircraft. *Courtesy Jean Borgatti.*

were required to open their purses and lunch containers for inspection on the way in and on the way out. Most of the workers boarded buses. Traffic in Niagara Falls near the war plants was extremely hectic at times. It was a cause of great concern. There were a lot of traffic accidents.

One Sunday morning, Jean was offered a ride home from the plant with a group of other female workers. Mrs. Glennie, an older woman, was the driver. On this occasion, Mrs. Glennie was thoroughly exhausted and accidentally fell asleep at the wheel. The automobile crashed into another automobile that was parked on the street in front of the Crown and Anchor Restaurant, at the corner of Pine Avenue and Twenty-ninth Street. Mrs. Glennie suffered chest injuries. Sophie Jakubek hurt her knees. Jean fractured her nose. Another woman, Jean's friend Kay Rotundo, was also slightly injured. Customers and staff from the restaurant came running outside to assist the women. They brought whatever rags they could find and used them to help stop their bleeding. The women were eventually taken to Memorial Hospital. Jean recalls that after being examined and having her nose packed, she and Kay were released. They walked all the way home, for

A female war worker at Bell Aircraft. *Courtesy Niagara Aerospace Museum and Archives.*

neither of the women had money for a cab. Phoning home was not possible, anyhow, as neither of their parents owned a telephone. But they were all right, and the following day, they worked another shift at Bell Aircraft.

The Art of War

During the war years, Bell Aircraft utilized innovative methods in order to increase production. One of these methods involved using art along the assembly lines. Well-known local artist Tony Sisti was recruited for the job. The nephew of one of Niagara Falls' most beloved priests, Monsignor Tronolone of St. Joseph's Roman Catholic Church, Sisti was hired to organize the first ever visual training program in a war plant. He was made to create large sketches of the aircraft industry showing male and female workers at the Bell Aircraft plant doing their jobs. His drawings were considered to be "the most complete layout of documented history of aircraft building in existence."[145]

Sisti drew about one hundred scenes in a series of pencil drawings. The sketches were supposed to help visually teach the workers, many of whom had never worked in such a job before, how to do their specific task. Apparently they fulfilled their purpose, as production "was greatly increased."[146]

During the time he worked on these sketches, he also taught art classes to more than one hundred Bell employees. Organized by request of the workers themselves, who had observed him as he worked on his sketches, the classes were quite successful. Most of the students were beginners and saw the classes as enjoyable and a relaxing alternative to time spent on the wartime assembly lines. They worked on charcoal and pencil portrait and still life drawings and in both watercolors and oils.

Camp Bell

Camp Cataract was officially formed on April 13, 1942, at the historic Cataract House hotel. It came together practically overnight. The entire facility was taken over by the Bell Aircraft Corporation on behalf of the army air forces in order to immediately quarter five hundred enlisted men who would train as aircraft mechanics. Civilian residents were evacuated,

Camp Bell instructors. *Courtesy Niagara Aerospace Museum and Archives.*

and the rooms were refitted for the purposes of the army camp. The elegant first-floor parlors were converted into classrooms where aircraft mechanics were taught in earnest. Even the ballroom was utilized, as it was changed into a makeshift hangar. Two Airacobras were set up for shop work. The original school supervisor was Louis Jewell.

In November 1942, Camp Cataract moved to Camp Bell. The new site, adjacent to the Niagara Falls Airport, had barracks, hangar space, a dining hall, a recreation building and an administration building. The entire operation was a joint venture between the Army Air Forces Technical Training Command and the Service Department of Bell Aircraft Corporation. It was under the command of Captain Cecil W. Henderson, commanding officer at the Bell Aircraft Training School, and A.L. Fornoff, head of Bell Aircraft's Service Department. Carl Diehl acted as supervisor of service training for the academy. All this was carried out under the direction of Major Peak.

The men who reported to Camp Bell came from army schools and had previously learned the basic elements of aircraft principles. At Camp Bell, they underwent five weeks of intensive training as P-39 Airacobra (and eventually P-63 Kingcobra) specialists. There were five classes in session

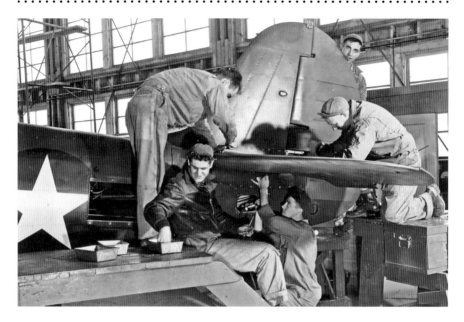

GI mechanics learning their trade at Camp Bell. *Courtesy Niagara Aerospace Museum and Archives.*

daily, and they were divided into two shifts. The first ran from 8:00 a.m. until 4:00 p.m. The second ran from 4:00 p.m. until 12:30 a.m. Each Tuesday, eighty-eight mechanics left the school, and on Thursdays of the same week, they were replaced by eighty-eight new students. The courses ran twenty-seven days and were taken in parts. For nine days, the students participated in lectures and demonstrations by Bell service instructors in academic classrooms. The next nine days were spent in practical shop work on the Airacobra equipment in laboratory classrooms. The final nine days were held in the hangars, in the Bell modification center, in the teardown department and on the flight line.

In February 1943, Camp Bell was awarded the efficiency banner of the First District AAFTTC for the quarter ending on December 31, 1942. It was the first time the banner was awarded to a school in the First District operated by an aircraft manufacturer.

Private Harry Middleton Jr., a graduate, made the following statement to the *Buffalo Courier Express*:

> *Personally, I think it's quite a trick to make a mechanic out of a man who doesn't even know how to hold a wrench when he starts. What helped us, I know, was the way they showed us how important it is to have a good*

ground crew for every airplane. When we realized that it takes up to twenty men on the ground to keep one combat plane in the air, we buckled down and really went to town. On the Niagara Frontier, where they teach us how to keep the Airacobras perking, they tell us about the way Larry Bell, head of the company, thinks about ground crews. "An airplane that's grounded isn't worth a damn" he says. "That's why we've got to have good maintenance men!"—And he's right, too.[147]

THE STORY OF THE "OLD 098"

When the "Old 098" finally took to the skies over Niagara, there was much cause for celebration. The Airacobra seemed a hopeless cause when it arrived at Camp Bell. It had been termed a total loss after a wreck in February 1942. The landing gear was damaged, the underside of the fuselage was a mess of twisted metal and the propeller was in ruins. More than one hundred other parts were seemingly mangled beyond repair. Supervisor Russ Miller, however, was hopeful that his mechanics would be able to bring it back to life and that it would one day fly again. And it did. After a year of repairs and being worked on by more than three hundred mechanics, it was in the air in October 1943. The work went on day and night. It seemed never-ending. They reduced the plane to a skeleton and basically rebuilt it from the bottom up.

The newspaper poetically described how the "deep throated roar of her powerful motor voiced the feelings of the men" who had made this event possible.[148] After returning from a successful flight, Lieutenant Beitner was pleased with the work that had gone into saving the plane.

"Tell the boys they did a fine job," he said to the officers and instructors. "098 is ok."[149]

THE END

In November 1944, the last graduating class of ground mechanics was received at a celebration held at the Red Coach Inn. Following the graduation, the camp was inactivated as part of an army air forces general program for curtailing schooling of aircraft maintenance men. The army air forces reported the number in the service was "sufficient to meet expected needs."[150] The last group included the 7,432nd man to graduate, Staff Sergeant James W. Fransisco.

WHEN LOVE WAS IN THE AIR

Oftentimes Niagara Falls is the setting for romance. Camp Bell was no exception. On March 19, 1944, Ethel Mt. Pleasant and Private Walter F. Zomont were married in Camp Bell's mess hall. The two had forged a wartime love affair after having met at the camp. Ethel served as a dietitian in the cafeteria. Private Zomont was a student training with the AAFTTC.

The wedding was a public celebration. Private Zomont, whose ancestry was Cherokee, and Ethel Mt. Pleasant, who was a member of the Bear clan of the Tuscarora Nation, shared Native American wedding customs. Their marriage brought together two Native Americans from different parts of the country in a unique ceremony that combined many family and tribal traditions with modern ones. The groom wore his military uniform and the bride wore a traditional wedding gown; however, members of her family and clan were clothed in native dress for the event.

MUSEUM AND ARCHIVES

The Bell Aircraft plant located at Niagara Falls played a significant role in the nation's wartime aviation story and was officially designated as a historic aerospace site in October 2012 by the American Institute of Aeronautics and Astronautics (AIAA). Today, the Niagara Aerospace Museum, located at the Niagara Falls International Airport at 9900 Porter Road, celebrates western New York's aerospace history, with great emphasis on the legacy of Bell Aircraft. The museum was first organized as a tax-exempt corporation under the State Education Department and opened to the public in May 1998 in the Summit Park Mall. The aircraft and aerospace artifacts had been acquired from the Amherst Museum by a group of aviation enthusiasts. After establishing itself in several different locations, the museum finally found a home at a former terminal at the Niagara Falls International Airport. The Niagara Frontier Transit Authority maintains the building. The museum

The Niagara Aerospace Museum. *Courtesy Tim Baxter.*

opened at this location in 2013. It is considered the most appropriate location as it is very close to the old Bell Aircraft factory.

The museum displays numerous historic artifacts in meticulously created exhibits. Its focus is on western New York's many contributions to aerospace history. Some of the aircraft on display include a Bell P-39 Airocobra that was raised from a lake in Russia, a 1910 Curtiss Pusher replica, the Bell Model 47 (the first United States commercially licensed helicopter), a Bell Rocket Belt, a Bell Lunar Accent Engine, the actual control panel used by a mission controller during the Apollo moon missions, the Bell X-22A (on loan from the National Museum of Naval Aviation) and a Curtiss JN-4 (Jenny).

The museum's library and archives are stored in the former Bell Aircraft plant. The collection includes thousands of historical documents, records, photos and books. The museum also houses an extensive film archives that has been digitized.

Chapter 7

WARTIME WORK IN NIAGARA FALLS

For some, wartime factory work was equally as hazardous as the battlefields of Europe or the Pacific. Many of the chemical plants processed materials known to be deadly. Daily exposure to lethal substances was quite common. There were very few safety measures in effect. When safety precautions were finally implemented many years later, it was often too late.

By the spring of 1943, half of all the workers in Buffalo and Niagara Falls worked in defense-related jobs.[151] The war brought forth an unprecedented number of jobs to the area. It produced an all-time high of forty-seven thousand jobs.[152] Many of the workers were young men and women. Some were too old to be considered for military service. They all understood that they were working with dangerous materials, but they probably were not able to comprehend the lasting effects of their wartime contact with these substances. They only knew that all Americans had been called forth to sacrifice for the cause of victory, and this was how they would contribute. Of course, the factories offered good-paying jobs to these men and women, and jobs were something that everyone who had survived the Great Depression was thankful for.

The CARB**O**WHEEL

THE EMPLOYEES' NEWS-MAGAZINE OF THE CARBORUNDUM COMPANY, NIAGARA FALLS, N.Y.

Making Ammunition for
the Production Front

Volume 1   **July, 1943**   **Number 7**

Female workers making ammunition for the front. *From the* Carbo Wheel, *Carborundum Company.*

MAJOR FACTORIES AND THEIR PRODUCTS

Niagara Falls had been a major industrial player since the 1920s. In fact, by 1925, the city was considered the "electro-chemical and electro-metallurgical center of the world."[153] According to the 1925 census, there were 116 industrial establishments in the city of Niagara Falls; 21 of these were chemical plants.[154] During World War II, Niagara Falls provided essential war products. These products included smoke pots, flares, disinfectants (bleaching powder and chlorine), sodium sulfides, caustics, aluminum chloride (for lubricant industries), poisons and poisonous gases, magnesium and other chemicals used in medicines, dyes, plastics, water repellants, soap, rayon and other synthetic materials. Several companies such as Hooker, Linde Air, DuPont, Olin, Hercules, National Lead, Union Carbide and Carborundum did secret work in conjunction with the United States Army Corps of Engineers for the Manhattan Engineering District Project. The Manhattan Project designed and built the first atomic bombs that were dropped on the Japanese cities of Hiroshima and Nagasaki at the end of the war.

The Chemical Warfare plant, located on Buffalo Avenue, was managed by the E.I. DuPont de Nemours Company. It was in full operation by December 1941. This plant employed about 140 workers and produced defense chemicals such as activated carbon and soda lime. The purpose of these materials was to safeguard American troops in the event of a chemical attack. Activated carbon is a dense form of charcoal that has the ability to absorb gases. Soda lime is an alkaline material, usually in granule form, that neutralizes acid fumes. Hexamethylenetetramine and other organic substances were also explored. There were often situations that arose when poisonous gases were released from this plant. Residents from an area around the Echota neighborhood complained to the city on a number of occasions. They were concerned that all the vegetation around their homes had died after exposure to these gases. In 1943, 205 dead trees were removed from this section of the city.[155] At the war's end, when the demand for these products had diminished, the workers were released and absorbed by the Electro-Chemical department of the E.I. DuPont de Nemours plant.

The Vanadium Corporation professed that its plant was "as much a battlefront of victory as the islands of the South Pacific or the plains of Russia."[156] This plant, located near Packard Road, employed more than five hundred men who worked three shifts daily in order to keep the furnaces running twenty-four hours per day. Raw ore was put through the

A war worker at Vanadium. *From "Soldiers of Production," the Vanadium Corporation of America.*

furnaces and released as a purified alloy metal. This substance would be used by the steel and iron makers to manufacture products such as armor plate, armor-piercing shells or parts for bomber planes.

During the 1940s, the Electrometallurgical Company, a subsidiary of the Union Carbide and Carbon Corporation, conducted uranium operations

PICTURED ABOVE ARE ED SHRUBSALL AND HIS RESEARCH DEVELOP-
MENT GROUP. Left to right, back row: E. Shrubsall, L. Stoyell, F. Gould, R. Mullen,
W. Mensinger, W. Clark, C. Elstrodt, C. O'Neill, W. Stevenson, P. Starnes, R. Hawkes,
F. Stevens, L. Heim. Second row: J. Morganti, H. Miller, J. D'Anna, C. Pollock,
E. Jierski, D. Firth, A. Malinowski, M. Scindle, D. Burden, J. Schmidt, S. Wolosin, F.
Wendt. Third row, sitting: L. Bonanni, T. Hearn, G. Bool, T. Sturgeon, G. Cracknell, J.
Hrybinczak, J. Stancombe. Front row: A. Williams, W. J. Yaggie, R. Sparkes, E.
Adamson, G. Heinrich, W. Murphy, M. Patterson, J. Thomson.

Workers from the Electrometallurgical Company. *From* The Tapping Pot,
Electrometallurgical Company.

at a location south of Pine Avenue and east of its intersection with Packard
Road. The initial furnace operations for uranium processing began in April
1943 and continued until August 1946 in three shifts per day. The company
produced uranium metal by reducing uranium tetrafluoride with magnesium
metal under high temperatures. The Electrometallurgical Company also
provided products for the steel and metal industries.

The Carborundum Company, located at 1920 Buffalo Avenue, was
founded on September 21, 1891, following the discovery of a substance
called silicon carbide. Silicon carbide, or carborundum, was found to be an
excellent abrasive material and was used on grinding wheels, sharpening
stones and sandpaper. The first plant opened in Niagara Falls in 1895.
Thanks to the abundant supply of electricity, the company was able to build
several high-powered furnaces to aid in processing. During World War II,
Carborundum was involved with various phases of the Manhattan Project.
The work done for this included conducting programs to determine suitable
methods for engineering and shaping uranium rods. They also formed,
coated and canned uranium rods. Workers at the Carborundum factory
in Niagara Falls "turned uranium billets into finished slugs for use in the
Clinton and Hanford piles."[157] Workers' exposure to hazardous materials

The Carborundum plant at Niagara Falls. *Courtesy Library of Congress.*

was inevitable. The centerless-grinding testing produced "significant levels of airborne radioactivity creating an inhalation and ingestion hazard."[158] The Carborundum Company was one of the city's largest employers. In fact, by the end of the war, 20 percent of Niagara Falls' workers were employed by Carborundum.[159]

The Hooker Electrochemical Company, located at 4700 Buffalo Avenue, another larger company in Niagara Falls, was established in 1903. Niagara Falls was found to be attractive as it provided low-cost electricity, and nearby mines could provide an abundance of salt. There was also a water source. Hooker grew from a small organization that produced a handful of chemical products to one of the country's substantial producers of heavy chemicals. During World War II, it produced more chlorine than any other American company. Hooker was also a leading supplier of dodecyl mercaptan, for the synthesis of rubber. Other products produced by Hooker during the war years were arsenic trichloride (used in poisonous gas), bleaching powders (decontaminants) and hexachlorobenzene (used in landing flares). By January 1943, Hooker had begun to provide assistance for the top-secret Manhattan Project. The plant manufactured fluoridated and chlorinated organic chemicals with byproduct hydrochloric acid. This was used in the chemical processing of uranium. It also manufactured pesticides and petrochemicals.

The legacy of Hooker and many of these other wartime production plants is a haunting presence in Niagara Falls, even today. Hooker was the principal company that dumped waste into the Love Canal site. Over 21,800 tons of at least two hundred different chemicals that were used for chlorinated hydrocarbons, pesticides, plastic residues and chemical sludge were dumped between 1942 and 1952.[160] The City of Niagara Falls and the United States Army also used the Love Canal site for dumping. Parts of the Manhattan Project were buried there as well. Over the years, after a neighborhood was built on the dump site, a major environmental crisis was at hand. There were mysterious odors and strange substances leaching from the ground in basements, backyards and the schoolyard. The Love Canal Home Owners Association conducted a study and found that the Love Canal neighborhood had an increase in miscarriages (300 percent greater risk in the "wet areas"), stillbirths, crib deaths, nervous breakdowns, hyperactivity, epilepsy and urinary tract disorders.[161] On August 7, 1978, President Jimmy Carter declared Love Canal a federal health emergency. He called for the allocation of immediate funds for cleanup and ordered the Federal Disaster Assistance Agency to assist the City of Niagara Falls. This was a momentous event in American history, as federal emergency funds had never before been used in a situation that was not a natural disaster.

Niagara Falls' industrial plants and wartime workers played a vital role during World War II. Many individuals worked on dangerous processes for the war effort. The toxic chemicals left behind are still a concern in Niagara Falls neighborhoods.

WARTIME TRAGEDIES OF THE HOOKER CHEMICAL COMPANY

Oftentimes, the youngest men were required to work at the chemical plants as part of the war effort. They were too young for the military, but they could serve in a different manner until their numbers were called.

Howard Woodcock began working at Hooker Chemical when he was just eighteen years of age. Two of his brothers served in the military. Howard probably imagined that his time would come soon as well. But when his order to report for induction arrived, he was too ill to join the other men on the bus trip to Buffalo. Instead, his father had to drive him. He was only nineteen years old, and he could not pass his physical exam. There would be no army life for Howard Woodcock.

"He was shot…after one year at Hooker," Howard's brother Harold Woodcock said.[162] He was not shot with a rifle though. His young body was wrecked by the dangerous chemicals he had worked with as a part of the war effort in Niagara Falls. Howard suffered from arsenic poisoning. The arsenic took all the fluid from his joints and left him barely able to stand without assistance. He suffered from lifelong ailments related to his year at Hooker. Eventually, his family found a doctor who specialized in chemical-related health issues in the Buffalo area. No physicians in Niagara Falls were able to help him.

Harold still remembers a number of his friends and his brothers' friends who also suffered from various exposures to harmful substances at the war plants. "These guys had no idea what they were dealing with," he remarked. Some of the men stayed in the plants for seven days at a time. They even slept there. "Most of those guys barely made it to their thirtieth birthdays. They died from these chemicals."

Joe Paonessa was a teenager when the war broke out in 1941. In 1943, just as he turned sixteen, his uncle, who was a foreman at Hooker, helped him get a job at the plant. The son of Italian immigrants, Joe was thrilled to get a good job in one of Niagara Falls' factories. In 1945, Joe's uncle asked him and a few of the other boys if they would be interested in volunteering for something very important. They were to meet in the main office. Joe agreed. Upon entering the office and seeing the army representatives, he realized that somehow this volunteer work would involve the war. It would just be a "finish-and-go-home" type of job, they told him.[163] He and the others said that they would do it.

The job was to open up twenty-five barrels that had been shipped in from another location. It seemed simple enough. The substance they were instructed to dump from the barrels looked like a white- or yellow-colored rock. Upon opening the barrels, they would dump the contents onto the floor and shovel it through a grate onto a conveyer belt. There would be quite a bit of dust. Whatever was left over would be scraped and put back into the barrels. Joe started thinking that they could finish much quicker if they dumped it right onto the conveyer. But because they were working quicker than expected, the army upped the number of barrels.

There was a system they were taught to follow. In the morning, they were told to put work clothes on and then to go to the first aid station to have a special cream applied over their entire bodies. They would then be given a special protective uniform. They would stop working at about 11:20 a.m. At this point, they were directed to shower and put other clothes on while they ate their lunch. When they would return for the afternoon shift, they would have to start the procedure all over again. They would head to the first aid station for the cream and new coveralls. Joe and the others did this for five days a week for one year. The substance turned out to be uranium. Joe's work was part of the Manhattan Project.

Unfortunately, Joe did not escape this contact with uranium unharmed. Many years later, he was stricken with lymphoma. He suffered terribly, but he made it through his treatments. He was awarded a settlement as compensation for his hazardous work. "I was grateful for the money, but money can never give you back your life," he said.

AFRICAN AMERICAN WAR WORKERS

According to Dr. Michael Boston, World War II brought on the "Second Great Migration," in which significant numbers of African Americans shifted northward and even into the city of Niagara Falls, New York. By 1940, the African American population of Niagara Falls had nearly doubled in size to 975 individuals. Technical advances that involved the mechanization of cotton picking led to the end of sharecropping and therefore significant unemployment issues in the Deep South. Many of these former sharecroppers came to Niagara Falls to work in the war industries, and a significant number were from Alabama. Bloneva Bond, a Niagara Falls resident, stated that "local industries chartered buses to bring people from the south to Niagara Falls."[164]

African American workers were often placed in lower-level plant jobs because it was believed that "they could best cope with the intense heat generated by the local plants" such as Carborundum, Union Carbide, the Carbon Corporation, Hooker Chemical, Bell Aircraft, the Vanadium Company and others.[165]

Anderson and Joseph Williamson, who descended from generations of families of sharecroppers from South Carolina before moving to Niagara Falls, found work in the plants "difficult" but a "release from tenant farming."[166] They also enjoyed being paid on a regular basis. They worked in the dangerous "open hearth furnaces" at Union Carbide and sent money back to South Carolina so that their families could join them in Niagara Falls.

Theodore, Joseph's son, graduated from Niagara Falls High School in 1941. He labored as a machinist for Union Carbide until joining the United States Marine Corps in 1943. Following the war, he proceeded to attend Simmons Mortuary Science School in Syracuse, New York, and graduated in 1947. He officially established his own funeral home in Niagara Falls in 1959, located on Tenth Street. On March 17, 1960, he bought the Bell funeral home building located at 635 Main Street, renaming it Williamson Funeral Home. His mortuary business was the first one to be operated by African Americans in the city of Niagara Falls.

FEMALE WAR WORKERS

Five years ago it would have been as unthinkable that a girl would be taking her place on the crew of a paper machine as for her grandfather to approve of his granddaughter wearing trousers. Yet both of these impossibilities are happening today. Furthermore, our girls are wearing the pants and doing things formerly done by men without losing those feminine attributes that men so value in women.[167]

The Selective Service Act changed many things in the United States. Passed by Congress as the Burke-Wadsworth Act, it was signed into law by President Roosevelt on September 16, 1940. It was the first peacetime draft in United States history. Initially, all men ages twenty-one to thirty-six were required to register with their local draft boards. However, when the United States entered the war, this was updated. By December 1941, the president signed an executive order that provided for "the most effective mobilization and utilization of national manpower."[168] The Selective Service System was transferred to the War Manpower Commission and led by Chairman Paul V. McNutt. Voluntary enlistments were suspended. Men would be drawn into the military through their local draft boards. Men between the ages of eighteen and forty-five were subject to military service, and all men ages eighteen to sixty-five were required to register. Ten million American men were inducted into the military during World War II.

The War Manpower Commission looked to fill the jobs left by the men who had entered the service with female workers. It was estimated that there were forty-two million women in the United States between the ages of eighteen and sixty-five. Fifteen million of these women were already employed, and four million of those employed were war workers. McNutt wanted to increase this number to six million.[169]

The Niagara Falls Mill of the Kimberly-Clark Corporation was representative of the situation at many of the other factories. The percentage of female workers before the war was 25 percent. By mid-1943, 45 percent of its workers were women. Over 350 men had left the Niagara Falls Mill for military service. It was estimated that about 12 men would leave their jobs per month, and all of these would need to be replaced.[170] During the months of February and March 1943, payrolls of Niagara Falls plants revealed that 1,200 female workers had been hired during that two-month period alone.[171] The Womanpower Census, taken in February 1943, reported that 5,398 Niagara Falls women were willing to accept war work.[172] Women who

Female wartime guards at the Carborundum plant. *From the* Carbo Wheel, *Carborundum Company.*

expressed an interest in the war industry were referred to the United States Employment Service at 220 First Street. Trained personnel were there to answer any questions and to help guide them to the jobs they would be best suited to fill.

The Women's Recruiting Committee of the War Manpower Commission canvassed locally in Niagara Falls for female workers. Women, even those who had never worked outside the home, were proving themselves very capable of industrial work. Some had discovered the work to be "interesting" and the tasks assigned to them "not as difficult as [they] appeared."[173] In fact, in certain positions, women proved even more skilled than some men. A local industrialist reported that female crane operators in almost every instance had proven "more capable of moving ten tons of metal around than were the men who preceded them at the controls."[174] The citywide canvass to

Nan Hannagan doing door-to-door recruiting in hopes of encouraging Niagara Falls women to work in war plants. Photographed by Marjory Collins, 1943. *Courtesy Library of Congress.*

recruit female war workers began in earnest on April 20, 1943, and lasted two weeks. Sixteen women, all workers in local plants, made personal visits to the homes of interested Niagara Falls women. Even Monsignor Tronolone of St. Joseph's Roman Catholic Church encouraged the cooperation of Niagara Falls women.

The United States was calling women to serve just as vigorously as it was calling on men. Niagara Falls, being one of the key cities of the war industry, could not allow itself to be shut down. "Niagara Falls and Buffalo are as important to the American war program as the Krupp armament works are to Germany, as Birmingham's coal is to England, as the Caucasus oil is to Russia. Only if women take over the jobs calling for them can Niagara Falls do her part in this war, which is not by a long shot, yet won," the *Niagara Falls Gazette* stated in February 1943.[175]

Chapter 8

FORT NIAGARA

Fort Niagara, a most beautiful and historic site at the mouth of the Niagara River, has proudly flown the flags of three nations for over three hundred years. It was at one time a vital and strategic location. The dominant colonial power that controlled this section of land ultimately controlled access to the Great Lakes and, therefore, westward movement into the vast, uncharted heart of America.

The history of Fort Niagara began in 1679, when famed French explorer Robert de La Salle established a small post with a storehouse and stockade, known as Fort Conti. It burned in less than a year. Other military installations were thereafter established on the site of Fort Conti. Fort Niagara, with its famed "castle," was constructed by the French in 1726. One of the more significant events in the history of Fort Niagara included the nineteen-day siege in which the fort was taken from the French by the British in July 1759. It was finally handed over to the Americans in 1796. The French and Indian Wars brought a great deal of action to the fort. During the War of 1812, Fort Niagara was captured by the British. Following the Treaty of Ghent, Fort Niagara was again returned to the United States, and it has remained in American hands for two hundred years.

In the time since the War of 1812, Fort Niagara has intermittently been used by the army. It was an active military installation during World War I, serving as an officers' training camp. In June 1922, the Twenty-Eighth Infantry was posted at Fort Niagara. It became a local fixture of

Fort Niagara. *Courtesy Jacob Henry.*

the community. Many social events occurred at the post and energized the atmosphere around the village of Youngstown. In September 1940, residents were brokenhearted when it was reported that the Twenty-Eighth Infantry would be departing. But little did they know that just as the Twenty-Eighth Infantry was scheduled to leave, it would be replaced by an even greater amount of military activity. Senator James M. Mead, of Buffalo, reported that the War Department had shown some interest in Fort Niagara and was actually planning on using it "to maximum capacity"[176] in the near future for a military training program. Senator Mead predicted that Fort Niagara was being eyed by the government because it was centered in an important industrial area and included excellent training facilities. It could also accommodate mechanized equipment. Very quickly, Senator Mead's predictions became a reality.

RECEPTION AND INDUCTION CENTER

I don't know how many thousands of men were going through Fort Niagara every day, but if you ever saw coal going down a chute, that's the way they were moving them in and moving them out.

—*Philip Ingraham*[177]

Immediately upon official word from Washington affirming that Fort Niagara would be utilized by the Selective Service Program for the reception of selectees and that all youths selected from the western New York and northern Pennsylvania areas would be sent there for initial processing, plans were made to update the location.

The preliminary notion was that Fort Niagara would serve as a final clearinghouse for men before they were to be assigned to the different branches of the army. The men called in the draft would be cared for at the stations near their homes first and then sent to Fort Niagara, where they

An aerial view of Fort Niagara during World War II. *Courtesy Old Fort Niagara Association.*

The entrance at Fort Niagara. *From* Niagara Falls Gazette.

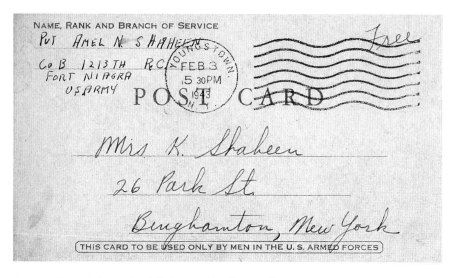

A postcard from inductee Amel Shaheen at Fort Niagara, February 3, 1943. *Author's collection.*

would be given uniforms, an introduction to military life and equipment. A board of army examiners also conducted a series of tests to help determine where the individual men would best serve.

Preparations to receive these men began in earnest during the winter of 1940–41. Over two hundred workers installed water and sewer mains in the area where the frame barracks were to be erected and at the south end by the Officers' Row. A new officers' quarters and mess hall were built, along with a twenty-foot road that connected the six two-story frame barracks and the two recreation halls. The processing building was enlarged, and a renovation of the Depression-era CCC buildings along the lake was also completed.

The 1213th Reception Center and the 1206th Service Union Station Complement (SUSC) were established following the passage of the National Guard and Reserve Act of the Selective Service Act of 1940. On December 6, 1940, 30 officers and 127 enlisted men with the 1213th Reception Center and the SUSC arrived at Fort Niagara from Fort Dix, New Jersey, in order to transform the fort into a processing center following the departure of the Twenty-Eighth Infantry. Colonel Floyd D. Carlock was in command of the post and the service unit. He was succeeded by Colonel Clay M. Supplee in January 1943.

The selectees were guided through the following processes: classification, a personal interview, a medical exam, a talk on government insurance programs and an issuance of army clothing. Upon arrival, they were each allotted a toilette kit containing a hairbrush and comb, a razor, soap and "everything a neat soldier needs."[178] Uniform items included the following: three wool undershirts, three pairs of wool drawers, three pairs of wool socks, two OD wool shirts, one pair of trousers, one pair of denim working trousers, one denim working jumper, one belt, one pair of service shoes, one wool coat, one wool overcoat, one raincoat, one field cap, one pair of OD wool gloves, four cotton handkerchiefs, one denim working hat, two EM collar insignia, one pair of leggings, one black necktie and one cotton khaki necktie. All of this was packed into a duffel bag.

The men were also introduced to army life and regulations through a series of lectures and films on war and military courtesy. They were briefly instructed in drill training and in arms training.

Contingents of about 150 men arrived daily. They would spend several days at Fort Niagara and then would be shipped off to training at another location. Some, however, were chosen to remain with the permanent garrison at Fort Niagara. During wartime, the fort had a population of about 1,200 men at any given time.

Selectees at Fort Niagara. *From* Niagara Falls Gazette.

Fort Niagara was an active scene during the war. In addition to serving as an induction center, the fort also was the setting for much amusement. Dances were a regular source of entertainment. There was at least one held per week. A new hall was constructed from the old clothing-issue building of the fort's former reception center and included facilities for dances, parties, plays, movies, wrestling, boxing and other events. A USO (United Service Organization) clubhouse was dedicated in December 1942. It contained a ping-pong table, a pool table, bridge tables, a radio, a recordio on which the soldiers were able to record letters to be sent home and many other games and amusements. There were sports teams that competed locally and a military band that was built up from selectees with previous musical training. The Fort Niagara band became one of the "outstanding musical organizations in Western New York."[179] The band led the Magna Charta parade at Niagara Falls, played at the Pioneer's Picnic at Olcott, broadcast weekly over WBEN radio, held regular concerts at the post and played for dances. An expanded library facility was opened in April 1944. Colonel Herbert D. Forrest, commanding officer, described it as an "arsenal" to equip its men with "knowledge of the cause they are defending."[180] The *Fort Niagara Drum*, the weekly enlisted men's newspaper, published stories, cartoons and relevant information. The staff was presented a loving cup in June 1944 during a special ceremony in which it was honored for winning the title as the best mimeographed newspaper of any service anywhere in the world. The *Fort Niagara Drum* won two years in a row.

In June 1943, Fort Niagara's mission was changed to that of a replacement-training unit. This lasted for only a few months, and then it served as a refresher unit for men of the Second Service Command. It was commanded by Major Paul J. Chesterton of the 1206th Service Command. Several of the men who were trained included combat veterans who had come from the front lines in North Africa. A fighter control squadron

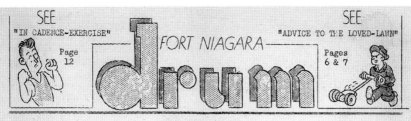

Vol. III, No. 22   FORT NIAGARA, N.Y.   July 9, 1943.

CAPTAIN BUSWELL NEW ADJUTANT

LIBRARY GETS FACE-LIFTING

Students, goldbricks, research experts and bookworms at Fort Niagara will have a veritable paradise in which to follow their pursuits when the remodeling and redecorating of the post library is completed next week.

The revamped literature emporium will be complete in every detail. Walls have been painted a baby blue, flowered drapes adorn the windows. The balcony has been removed, the ceiling dropped, new fixtures and floor lamps have been added. To top off the new setting, comfortable lounge furniture has taken the place of the chairs that were previously in use. No tome has been left unturned in making the Fort Niagara library one of the best in the entire Second Service Command. Daily papers from various cities will also be available. These include the New York Times, Tribune, Daily Mirror, PM and papers of surrounding localities.

Two Weekly Dances Planned For Post

Dance devotees at Fort Niagara will have no cause for griping if plans now being formulated by the Special Service Office materialize. A movement is now under way to stage two dances each week for permanent party men, instead of the customary one. Because of the growth of the permanent party two dances are really essential to satisfy the swingin' thirsts of our GI jivers. The new system may start next week.

ASSUMES DUTIES TUESDAY, JULY 6

Capt. Clark J. Buswell, Cav., added new duties to his list of assignments this week when he was appointed Post Adjutant and Adjutant of the 1264th Training Battalion. He will continue as Operations and Training Officer, Commander of Detachment and Detachment Headquarters and Range Officer.

Capt. Buswell, who came here from White Plains, New York, was formerly a member of the 317th Cavalry at Ft. Sheridan, Ill. Retiring as a first lieutenant in 1932, the Captain became associated with the Pillsbury Flour Mills Co. in New York City, acting as Sales Manager of the New York Division. He held that position until recalled to active duty at Fort Niagara, December 27, 1941. He has performed many duties since his arrival here. On October 17, 1942, he was promoted to Captain. Captain Buswell resides on the post with his wife and family.

Fort Niagara Drum, post newspaper, dated July 9, 1943. *Author's collection.*

was also organized to train enlisted men of the army air forces with radio equipment and sound detection devices. This squadron was commanded by Major G.E. Grimes. By April 1944, it had become a separation center under Colonel Herbert Forrest.

PRISONERS OF WAR

Perhaps one of Fort Niagara's most unique undertakings involved its use as a POW camp. As a consequence of the massive destruction caused by the war in Europe, there were few locations within the continent suitable for holding German POWs. The United States found it necessary to ship the prisoners to the United States on returning American ships. Initially, they were placed in Texas for temporary holding. By 1944, Fort Niagara had been chosen as an ideal site and given very short notice to prepare for their arrival.[181]

The first German prisoners arrived on June 12, 1944. They were mostly prisoners from Field Marshal Erwin Rommel's Afrika Korps. The POWs were brought by train and kept at the Depot Hotel in Niagara Falls. By the war's end, they numbered about 1,800 men. Later groups of prisoners included men who had been captured in France and at other locations through which American troops were advancing. Some of the POWs were not German but Russians who had been forced into conscription by the Germans. The prisoners ranged in age from eighteen to sixty-four.

German POWs arriving at Niagara Falls. *From* Niagara Falls Gazette.

The POW camp at Fort Niagara. *Courtesy Old Fort Niagara Association.*

At Fort Niagara, the POWs utilized more than fifty buildings, including sleep quarters, latrines, a mess hall, canteens and other structures. A three-thousand-foot fence was placed around the stockade. The prisoners were permitted to cultivate a twelve-acre farm in order to produce their own food. By doing so, demands on army-issued food were greatly reduced.

According to Colonel John M. McDowell, the commanding officer of the military district of New York, these prisoners would be "harbored under strict and rigorous conditions."[182] They were brought to Niagara County for nonmilitary tasks under terms of the Geneva Convention. They were actually quite vital to the Niagara area as farm workers. Congressman Walter Andrews worked with the Second Service Command at Governor's Island at procuring prisoners to work the fields in the fall of 1944. Due to the fact that there was a shortage of men, there simply were not enough hands to harvest the fruit crops. The POWs were transported to farms and work sites throughout the area and returned at night. Many of them had farming experience.[183] They pruned trees, harvested fruit and worked in canning factories and apiaries. For the most part, there was a very positive exchange between the prisoners and the local people they interacted with while working. There are many kind letters that area farmers received from these men after they returned to Germany.[184]

There were also a few tragedies. It was not all fun and games. One August day in 1945, Karl Freudenstein, age thirty-three, committed suicide by hanging in the barn on the Edward O. Hurtgam farm on Frog Hollow Road, near Ransomville. It was believed that he was "mentally depressed."[185] He was buried in the Fort Niagara Cemetery.

The prisoners were returned to Europe by November 1945. Some were reported as having "wept openly" at the news.[186] A group stayed behind in order to aid in the preparation of the abandonment of the post by the army on December 31, 1945.

ABANDONMENT AND NEW LIFE

Thousands of men were lucky enough to first experience army life at the beautiful and celebrated Fort Niagara. It was said that some of the new draftees may have "experienced a spiritual tie with his country's military past as he gazed upon Old Fort Niagara and learned something of its history."[187]

When the time came that the army had no more use for the fort, many local residents were saddened. Some saw that it was inevitable. According to a poll taken by the *Niagara Falls Gazette* in September 1945, locals were split down the middle. Half were in favor of eliminating the fort as a military post, and the other half favored the post remaining.[188] By December, a surplus commodity sale was held at Fort Niagara. Medical equipment, household items, garden tools, lumber supplies and more were auctioned off to the highest bidder. It seemed that it was truly the end.

At midnight on December 31, 1945, the property was turned over to the custody of the army's district engineers to await final disposition. Many suggestions as to its future use were proposed. Some felt it could serve as temporary housing to help relieve the housing crisis that existed during the postwar years. Others felt it could be transformed into a rest center for war veterans or even a university.

The military abandonment had no effect on Old Fort Niagara itself, which had been taken over by the Old Fort Niagara Association in 1926. It was not too long afterward, though, that the fort was put to use as a military installation once again, for the Korean War resulted in troops being stationed at the site.

The last military troops were officially withdrawn in 1963. Except for the United States Coast Guard, which is stationed below the fort, the military history of Fort Niagara is something of the past.

Today, Old Fort Niagara celebrates its glorious military history. It is operated by the Old Fort Niagara Association, Inc., in cooperation with the New York State Office of Parks, Recreation and Historic Preservation.

Chapter 9

RATIONING, WARTIME COOKING AND RECIPES FROM NIAGARA FALLS

For many Americans, Niagarans included, wartime cooking was not a far stretch from the manner in which they prepared food during the meager Depression years. The immigrant families who made up a large portion of the population of the city of Niagara Falls had mostly grown their own fruits and vegetables since arriving. They utilized every plot of earth around their homes for food production. They grew grapes, beans, peas, zucchini, tomatoes, peppers, lettuce, assorted herbs and figs. They made homemade wine, bread and sausages and fermented and pickled foods. Some Niagarans kept chickens or rabbits for ready meat. The Italians foraged for edible greens such as dandelions and cardoons. During the spring months, they ventured out into the countryside, or even along highways, in order to dig up these healthful and delectable plants. During the war years, when healthy but simple meals prepared with homegrown ingredients were encouraged, Niagara Falls was well prepared.

However, it was inevitable that rationing would create many headaches for the homemaker, for some items were not available for purchase at times. In fact, for those who were dependent on canned goods, there was actually an eight-day period in which "narry [*sic*] a can of fruits or vegetables could be sold legally anywhere in the United States" before rationed sales began.[189] Once the point rationing system was worked out and the rules established, the market was reopened. There were also times when meat was scarce. The United States Army took 60 percent of the US Choice grade cuts of beef.

The ration card of Emilio Settimi, Niagara Falls. *Author's collection.*

In March 1943, when meat rationing was first introduced, Americans were asked to cut meat consumption to eleven pounds per person, per year.[190] In March 1944, an acute "Meat Emergency" was declared in nearby Buffalo. The chamber of commerce was compelled to wire the Office of Price Administration (OPA) urging that full responsibility for the local situation "be placed in the hands of the local OPA."[191] The shortage of beef, veal and lamb was acute. Twenty-five small meatpackers had announced that they would close their doors until the OPA took steps to ensure that they could "sell meat before incurring a loss."[192]

Luckily for America, there were creative ways to deal with the shortages. Peggy Taylor Hulligan recalls her excitement as a young girl when her mother would ask her to "color the margarine." Butter substitutes, such as Cudahy's Delrich Vegetable Margarine, included "an e-z color pak," or a capsule with red dye that needed to be pinched and then worked through the margarine. "It tasted awful," she said, but that was all her family had at times.[193]

VICTORY GARDENS

Let's raise vegetables at home so our boys can raise hell with our enemies abroad.
—*True N. Hewitt*[194]

As part of the war effort, the United States government encouraged people to plant Victory Gardens. Emphasis was on making Americans self-sufficient and therefore reducing the need for canned goods and prepackaged food items, which were necessary for shipment to our troops and our allies.

Victory Gardens were planted in backyards, in empty lots and even on rooftops. Niagara Falls' exertions were often commended. John L. Stockey, of the United States Department of Agriculture and coordinator of the Niagara County Victory Garden Council, said that area organizations "endeavored to have every foot of available soil planted so that Niagara Falls can say that this important war activity is 'well in hand.'"[195] The Niagara Falls Power Company made forty-eight lots available, each about fifty square feet, directly opposite the plant on Buffalo Avenue. Gardens were springing up in many unique locations.

By October 1943, the Niagara County Victory Garden Council declared that approximately 1,650 Victory Gardens had been established within the city of Niagara Falls. This number rose to 5,300 by 1944. The New York State College of Agriculture at Cornell University praised Niagarans and said that the Niagara County Victory Garden Council was "one of the most successfully operated councils of its kind in the state."[196] On another occasion, it also remarked that "Niagara Falls gardeners produced some of the finest gardens in New York State."[197] Two industries from Niagara County were honored by being awarded National Victory Garden Institute plaques "for superior employee garden promotion": the Wurlitzer Company at Martinsville and the Niagara Falls Power Company.

True N. Hewitt, director of the Industrial and Convention and Visitors' Service at the Chamber of Commerce building, served as the local representative. Fred White was the chairman of the Niagara Falls Victory Garden Council and president of the Niagara Falls Garden Club.

It was envisioned that the efforts would continue even after the war and that Niagara Falls would also be known "as a city of beautiful vegetable gardens and beautiful flower gardens."[198]

Popular Wartime Cookbooks

Cookbooks were published and sold all over the country that presented budget meals for wartime. Josephine Gibson's *Wartime Canning and Cooking Book*, a sixty-four-page volume, contained point-saving recipes for good, nutritious meals. Advertised in the *Niagara Falls Gazette*, it revealed that "you can eat well though rationed" if you use this cookbook.[199] The newspaper arranged to have sufficient copies available for "everyone in Niagara Falls and vicinity." Readers desired most of all to learn of

Kerr Home Canning Book. National Nutritional Issue, Food for Victory. *Author's collection.*

substitutes for rationed foods, recipes for meatless meals, directions for preserving and canning, methods of stretching meat and butter and new ways to prepare balanced meals.

Other popular cookbooks and pamphlets in the Niagara Falls area included *National Nutritional Issues* for the Food for Victory program. The *Kerr Home Canning Book*, released in 1942, stated that according to a recent National Nutrition Conference, a "challenge was given to every one of the 28 million homemakers of America in the following recommendation: *It is vital for the United States to make IMMEDIATE USE of the newer knowledge of NUTRITION in the present NATIONAL EMERGENCY. To neglect this would be as hazardous as to neglect military preparedness.*"[200] In other words, according to the Kerr Company, canning was imperative to winning the war. This pamphlet was designed to "meet the need of the hour" and to encourage health.[201] Assistance with canning, including special canning demonstrations, was provided in local neighborhood centers in Niagara Falls. On August 25, 1943, Miss Edna Seyffer, Urban Emergency Home Demonstration agent of the nutrition committee of the Niagara Falls War Council, conducted demonstrations, including "up-to-the-minute information concerning the new types of jar tops."[202]

Short Cuts and Left-Overs, by Hannah W. Schloss, originally published in 1938 and printed once again in 1942, was a national bestseller as it served as a Depression day reminder to leave nothing for waste—especially during wartime. The new red-white-and-blue-striped cover was appealing to homemakers and stressed the fact that home economy was vital to the war effort and the "watchword for victory."[203] It called on the American housewife to accept her own special patriotic duties, which included stretching the food supplies and creating healthy meals to keep her family robust and strong.

THE VICTORY COOKBOOK CONTEST

As part of a nationwide effort to educate young women on the "importance of war-time menus which use inexpensive and surplus foods, but at the same time present balanced diets for the war workers," the Niagara Falls Chapter of the Daughters of the American Revolution (DAR) sponsored a Victory Cookbook contest in 1943 for "girl homemakers," ages twelve to eighteen.[204] Due to the fact that there were "fewer canned, packaged and processed food available," it was stated that "more vegetables, cereal food, soups and meat dishes must originate in home kitchens."[205] Several local schools and organizations took part, and many entries were made.

As a result of the contest, it was announced that the Niagara Falls Chapter had won a state prize for the "greatest amount of worthwhile war work done by the Homemakers group."[206] More than six hundred young women from Niagara County created 149 cookbooks. They submitted 3,400 individual recipes from sixteen different schools, clubs or youth organizations. Throughout the competition, 4 members from each group appeared twice a week on the *Kitchen Korner* radio program on WHLD out of Niagara Falls. They shared recipes and discussed the Food for Freedom program. From the sixteen groups, 3 recipes were chosen and sent to Washington, D.C., for entry in the national contest. The Victory Cookbooks were on display throughout the week of March 16, 1943, at the Niagara Hudson building.

Recipes from fifteen area contestants were selected for publication in the 1943 *Girl Homemakers' Cookbook*, published by the National Chapter, DAR, in Washington, D.C. Some of the winning recipes from the area included a spice cake recipe submitted by Elizabeth Grafuis, Niagara Falls Girl Scouts; Sailor's Duff by Julia Niewistewicz, Trott Vocational School homemaking classes; chicken pie with vegetables by Ruth Jacklin, also of Trott Vocational School homemaking classes; Creole corn, submitted by Thelma Sutherland, Cloverleaf Club of the YWCA, Girl Reserves; Yankee Doodle Chow Mein by Ann Watson, seventh grade troop, Junior Catholic Daughters; meat squares à la mode and vegetable smothered liver, homemaking classes at Barker High School; shepherd's pie by Diane Hopkins, Wilson High School; corn and sausage casserole by Ann Thompson, Newfane High School; Orange Fool by Margaret Shellbury, also Newfane High School; Victory casserole by Dorcas Duncan, Lewiston High School; sausage apple casserole by Joan Maurer, Fenton Grammar school, North Tonawanda; baked fish pie and apple meringue by homemaking classes, Lockport High School; and honey-blueberry cake by A. MacEvoy, 4-H Club Orangeport Rangers.

The cookbook was for sale at the Niagara Hudson building through Miss Jessie McConnell or by phoning Mrs. George J. Reichert, regent of the Niagara Falls Chapter, DAR.

"MENUS OF THE DAY"

Mrs. Alexander George, an Associated Press food editor, was perhaps one of the more significant influences on Niagara Falls cooking during the war. In addition to being carried by the *Niagara Falls Gazette*, her column also appeared in newspapers throughout the country. Her daily "Menus of the Day" provided uncomplicated recipes that fit within the current wartime food situations. George shared important kitchen tips regarding saving fuel and recycling ingredients as well. She imparted nutritional information, meat alternatives and cleaning advice. Many of George's

Recipes from Mrs. George. *From* Spokane Daily Chronicle, *May 17, 1940.*

recipes had point-rationed items "starred" and involved low cost or non-rationed ingredients. Most were quick and easy to prepare but high in nutritional value. Her columns taught the American cook to look at mealtime with new eyes. When meat was rationed, she promised it would be "no bugaboo" to the "alert homemaker"[207] for, thankfully, with such "American standbys as cheese, eggs, beans, peas, nuts and other meat alternatives in the nutrition for victory program," we would prevail during these difficult times. By 1943, she declared that there were plenty of palatable meals to be made with unrationed meats such as liver, kidney, calf's hearts and oysters.[208]

George made sure to remind her readers that staying strong and healthy was never more important. War workers at home needed to maintain a vigorous diet in order to ensure victory abroad. "Since more and more foods are being put on the ration list and almost everybody is working longer, a good stout breakfast is more than ever the most important meal of the day."[209] George declared once and for all that "skimpy, 'grab and gulp' breakfasts should be out for the duration."[210]

Mr. N.P. Anderson, chairman of the Offices of Civilian Protection, personnel director of the Union Carbide Company and head of the Niagara Falls War Council, validated George's sentiment by declaring the promotion of healthy diets imperative in a statement delivered in October 1942: "Now that we have a war to win, a day lost by an employee is a day's production lost for the man at the front."[211] He added that "nourishing food" makes for "less illness."[212] As a result of the findings of wartime studies, local companies began to install cafeterias for their employees in order to ensure that the workers under the strain of war production remained strong and healthy. Interestingly, Anderson also stated that in the heavy industries he had "seen men on the midnight shift use the heat of the huge furnaces to prepare a meal that would be the envy of the finest chef. Their stews, baked potatoes and steaks are truly something to remember."[213]

If only Mrs. Alex George had been able to share those recipes!

SAMPLES FROM "MENUS OF THE DAY"

Victory Garden Offerings

Niagara Falls Gazette, July 12, 1943
(Point-rationed items are starred)

Victory Potato Salad
1½ cups cubed cooked potatoes
½ cup diced carrots
½ cup cooked green beans
⅓ cup diced celery
2 tablespoons minced onions
1 tablespoon minced parsley
⅓ teaspoon of salt
⅓ teaspoon of paprika
2 tablespoons French dressing

Mix and chill ingredients. Add bacon dressing.

Bacon Dressing
1 teaspoon salt
1 teaspoon dry mustard
2 tablespoons sugar
¼ teaspoon paprika
¼ teaspoon celery seed
½ cup vinegar juice or lemon
1 cup salad oil
*3 tablespoons crisp bacon, crumbled

Mix together salt, mustard, sugar, paprika and celery seed. Add 2 tablespoons each of vinegar and oil. Blend well. Alternate rest of vinegar with oil. Beat 2 minutes with fork. Chill in covered jar. This dressing will keep a month stored in refrigerator. Mix 4 tablespoons dressing with the bacon and blend into the salad.

Victory Doughnuts

Niagara Falls Gazette, April 8, 1942
Molasses doughnuts come to rescue as sugarless sweet.

1 cup molasses
1 cup buttermilk
2 tablespoons fat, melted
2 eggs, beaten
1 teaspoon vanilla
1 teaspoon salt
1 teaspoon cinnamon
¼ teaspoon nutmeg
½ teaspoon ginger
5 cups flour
1 teaspoon soda
2 teaspoons baking powder

Mix molasses, buttermilk, fat and eggs. Beat a minute and add rest of ingredients. Roll out soft dough and cut doughnuts. Fry in deep fat until well browned on both sides.

.

Meatless Dinner (Serving 2 or 3)

Niagara Falls Gazette, October 26, 1942

Victory Salad Deluxe
1 tablespoon gelatin
¼ cup cold water
2 cups tomato juice
1 teaspoon finely chopped onions
¼ cup diced celery
1 tablespoon chopped green pepper
1 teaspoon minced parsley
½ teaspoon salt
¼ teaspoon paprika
¼ teaspoon sugar

1 tablespoon lemon juice

1 cup cottage cheese

Soak gelatin 5 minutes; simmer for 5 minutes the juice and seasonings. Pour over gelatin and stir until dissolved. Cool and add lemon juice. Thicken slightly and pour over cheese placed in shallow mold. Chill until firm. Unmold, cheese side up, and serve on lettuce, cut in squares. Spread with mayonnaise or salad dressing.

Victory Fruit Bread

2½ cups flour

1 teaspoon soda

2 teaspoons baking powder

1 teaspoon salt

1 cup bran cereal

1 cup strained honey

1 egg beaten

3 tablespoons fat, melted

1 cup orange juice

2 tablespoons milk

1 teaspoon grated orange peel

⅔ cup chopped apricots

1 teaspoon grated lemon rind

Beat ingredients thoroughly. Pour into loaf pan lined with 2 thicknesses of waxed paper. Bake 1¼ hours in moderately slow oven (325 degrees).

Peanut Butter Cup Cakes

Niagara Falls Gazette, April 21, 1942

⅓ cup fat

1 cup dark brown sugar

½ cup peanut butter

1 teaspoon vanilla

½ teaspoon salt

2 eggs, beaten

⅔ cup milk

2 cups cake flour
3 teaspoons baking powder
½ teaspoon cinnamon

Cream fat and sugar. Add ingredients and beat 2 minutes. Half-fill greased muffin pans. Bake 20 minutes in moderate oven.

Dinner in 35 Minutes

Niagara Falls Gazette, August 24, 1943
(Point-rationed items are starred)

Tomato Surprise (Meat Alternative)
4 large firm tomatoes
1 cup corn, cut from cob
⅔ cup bread cubes
2 tablespoons minced onions
2 tablespoons flour
⅓ teaspoon salt
¼ teaspoon pepper
*2 tablespoons butter or margarine, melted

Scoop out centers from tomatoes. Mix pulp with rest of ingredients. Stuff the tomatoes and arrange in shallow baking pan. Add ½ inch boiling water. Bake 35 minutes in moderate oven. Baste several times.

Sugarless Dessert

Niagara Falls Gazette, May 12, 1942

Here is a sugarless dessert: Cut grapefruit in halves. Discard seeds and cores. Loosen each segment with a sharp knife. Sprinkle with a dash of salt and lightly brush with melted butter. Broil until brown and bubbly on top. Put a little maple syrup in centers and serve immediately.

Noodle Cheese Loaf

Niagara Falls Gazette, June 13, 1942

2 cups cooked noodles or macaroni
1 tablespoon chopped onions
2 tablespoons chopped green peppers
1 tablespoon chopped parsley
1 tablespoon horseradish (prepared kind)
3 eggs, beaten
1 cup milk
½ cup soft breadcrumbs
⅔ cup grated yellow cheese
1 teaspoon salt
¼ teaspoon paprika

Mix ingredients and pour into buttered loaf dish. Bake in moderately slow oven (325) for an hour. Unmold and cover with tomato sauce.

Under Cover Cooking

Niagara Falls Gazette, January 23, 1942

Try this low cost main dish: Fill a shallow, greased baking dish with macaroni and cheese, bake 25 minutes in moderate oven, then cover with split frankfurters and bake 20 minutes, or until well browned.

Some Meats Unrationed Under New Plan May Become Palatable Meals

Niagara Falls Gazette, January 21, 1943

Stuffed Calf's Heart is filled with needed vitamins. Wash and discard veins and arteries from the heart—the butcher may do this for you. Stuff with your best savory filling and tie the heart together or peg with skewers. Sprinkle with flour and quickly brown on all sides in a small amount of fat heated in a frying pan. Transfer heart to casserole and add one cup water and $\frac{1}{2}$ cup chopped onions to the frying pan. Boil a minute and then pour over the heart. Sprinkle with one teaspoon salt, $\frac{1}{4}$ teaspoon each pepper and poultry seasonings. Cover and bake for two hours in moderately slow oven—about 325 degrees F. Uncover and bake ten minutes. Remove heart to serving platter and thicken the drippings by adding two tablespoons butter mixed with three tablespoons flour. Pour over the heart. Leftover heart can be chopped and made into cakes or meatloaf mixture or combined with vegetables and sauce for escalloping.

LOCAL WARTIME RECIPES FROM NIAGARA FALLS

Dandelion Salad

Courtesy Jean Borgatti

2 cups dandelion greens
3 large cloves garlic, chopped
$\frac{1}{4}$ cup extra virgin olive oil
1 tablespoon red wine vinegar
salt and pepper to taste

Wash dandelion leaves thoroughly under cold water. Pat dry with a clean towel. Remove tender leaves from tougher stems. Add garlic. Drizzle with extra virgin olive oil and vinegar. Salt and pepper to taste.

Cabbage Soup

Courtesy Jean Borgatti

onion, chopped
2 tablespoons olive oil
small cabbage, chopped
3 large potatoes, washed and peeled and cut into chunks
3 large carrots, washed and peeled and cut into chunks
ham bone (if you have one)

Fry onions in olive oil. Add cabbage. Add water to cover and bring to a boil. Add chopped and peeled potatoes and carrots. You can also add ham. Cook until vegetables are tender.

Fresh String Beans and Potatoes

Courtesy Eleanor Migliazzo Novara

2 large potatoes
1 pound fresh string beans, trimmed
¼ cup extra virgin olive oil (you will need more for drizzling over the finished mixture)
2 garlic cloves, peeled and sliced (with salt and freshly ground pepper)
½ onion, peeled and chopped
several sprigs of Italian parsley, chopped

Peel the potatoes and cut into 1½-inch pieces. Pour enough cold water over the potatoes in a large saucepan to cover by about 3 inches. Bring to a boil over high heat, lower heat to a gentle boil and cook about 8 minutes. Add the string beans and continue cooking until both are tender—about 7 or 8 minutes. Drain the vegetables in a colander. Heat ¼ cup olive oil in skillet over medium heat. Sauté the garlic and onion and cook until slightly browned, about 1 minute. Slide the drained potatoes and string beans into the skillet, season again (if needed) with salt and pepper and mix together. Drizzle additional olive oil into the vegetables and mix just before serving. Top with parsley. This dish can be served warm or cold.

Canned Eggplant

Courtesy Velma Di Marco

1 eggplant
salt
equal parts cider vinegar and water
olive oil to cover
sprinkle of oregano (to taste)
sprinkle of crushed red pepper (to taste)
1 small clove garlic, sliced

Cut eggplant into slices (¼ inch thick); salt and drain overnight. Mix equal parts cider vinegar and water and bring to a boil. Drop eggplant slices a little at a time in a pot. When it comes to a boil again, turn slices for 1 minute. Remove and place on paper towels to drain when all are cooked. Start to fill jars by putting a little olive oil on bottom of jars. Then layer eggplant. Season every layer with oregano, crushed red pepper and garlic (a small clove or slices). Fill jars with olive oil and cap. Refrigerate before serving.

Tomato Soup Cake

Courtesy Marcia Buzzelli

1 can tomato soup
1 teaspoon baking soda

Mix above in large bowl as it will foam up.

1 egg
4 tablespoons shortening
1 cup brown sugar
2 cups flour
3 teaspoons baking powder
1 teaspoon cinnamon
1 teaspoon nutmeg
½ teaspoon ground cloves
¾ cup raisins
½ cup nuts

Combine all ingredients and bake in 9x9 greased and floured pan at 350 degrees for 40 minutes.

Icing
1 cup powdered sugar
3 ounces cream cheese
a little milk to spread

VICTORY COOKBOOK CONTEST PRIZE RECIPES

Topsy Turvy Meat Pie

First Prize by Alice Dischinger, Troop 242, North Tonawanda

1 cup sliced onion
2 tablespoons fat
1 pound ground beef
1–4 teaspoons celery seed
1–2 teaspoons pepper
1 teaspoon salt
1 can tomato soup or home-canned tomatoes put through sieve
2 cups enriched flour
3 teaspoons baking powder
1–2 teaspoons salt
1–4 cups shortening
1 cup milk, approximately

Brown onions in hot fat in frying pan. Add meat. Cook until lightly browned and crumbly. Add seasonings and tomato soup, or tomatoes, and simmer until thick. Sift flour, measure and sift again with baking powder and salt. Cut in shortening. Add milk and mix well. Pour over hot meat. Bake in hot oven. Turn onto chop plate. Cut in wedges and serve hot.
Temperature: 450 degrees
Time: 20 minutes
Yield: 6–8 servings

Sausage Apple Casserole

Second Prize by Joan Maurer, Felton Grammar School

1 pound pork sausage links
3 large apples
3 medium sweet potatoes
1–3 cups brown sugar
2 tablespoons sausage drippings
1–4 cups boiling water

Cook sweet potatoes until tender, peel and slice. Pan-fry sausage slowly for ten minutes, pouring off fat as it rises. Core apples and slice. Arrange sausage, apples and sweet potatoes in greased casserole and sprinkle with sugar. Combine boiling water and two tablespoons fat from sausages and pour over mixture.

Temperature: 375 degrees

Time: 40 minutes

Yield: 6 servings

Louisiana Put-Together

Second Prize by Joan Maerten, Girl Scout Troop 371

3–4 pound flank steak or leftover beef roast
4 tablespoons shortening
3 onions sliced
1 green pepper, sliced
1 cup leftover cooked vegetables
1 cup diced celery
1 cup tomato soup
1½ teaspoons salt
⅛ teaspoon pepper
8 stuffed olives, sliced
1 cup steamed rice

Cut meat in very thin slices. Heat skillet, melt shortening, and fry meat rapidly until brown and crisp. Remove meat. Cook onion and pepper until soft. Add tomato soup, meat, celery and seasonings. Simmer until onions and celery are tender. Add leftover vegetables (peas, string beans or carrots) and olives. Serve with steamed rice. Yield: 6–8 servings

Chapter 10

VICTORY

THE END OF A TWO-FRONT WORLD WAR

On this Mother's Day, so soon after V-E Day, one feels more like weeping than celebrating, for the cost has been so great. My heart rejoices with mothers to whom comes a long-awaited promise of fulfillment; while I mourn with those who have given their all.
—Lora Marie McClint[214]

Perhaps nothing reveals the general sentiment that prevailed in Niagara Falls when victory in the European theater of conflict was officially declared on May 8, 1945, more than these lines penned by Lora Marie McClint. Although there was much joy as a result of President Truman and Prime Minister Churchill's radio addresses, the fact remained that it had been a very costly war. There was still much work to do. There were still loved ones in harm's way, and there was yet another war to win in the Pacific.

There had been initial plans to celebrate V-E Day by declaring a holiday from work at the war industries in Niagara Falls. However, this idea did not come to fruition. The general feeling was that there could be no real celebrating until there was victory over Japan. Our men in uniform were still fighting it out against the Japanese, and there would be no holiday for them. How could we betray our brothers, fathers, husbands and sons? In fact, the *Niagara Falls Gazette* was happy to report that "exceptional good attendance on the job and no stoppage of work to celebrate V-E Day off the job were reported in the large war industries [in] this city."[215]

NEW YORK STATE'S TENTH CITY—POWER CITY OF THE WORLD

Home Edition NIAGARA FALLS GAZETTE

VOL. LII—NO. 128 THIRTY-TWO PAGES NIAGARA FALLS, N. Y., WEDNESDAY, AUGUST 15, 1945 THIRTY-TWO PAGES PRICE THREE CENTS

Victory headline on August 15, 1945. *From* Niagara Falls Gazette.

There was definitely rejoicing from all corners of the city after 9:00 a.m., when President Truman's proclamation was heard through the local radio broadcasts. Church services were the biggest plan for Niagarans, as Masses of thanksgiving were planned for the evening.

Perhaps one of the other reasons it was hard to break out of the solemnity of the season was that the flags were still at half-staff in observance of the period of mourning following President Franklin Delano Roosevelt's untimely death on April 12, 1945. There was certainly happiness and relief and a feeling that the Allies were inching toward total victory, but most people in Niagara Falls were content to "wait until V-J Day" to finally celebrate.[216]

That day did finally come. On the evening of Tuesday, August 14, 1945, President Truman announced to the American people that the Japanese had surrendered. The Second World War was officially over, and this time, Niagara Falls was not in a state of somber reflection. Immediately after the president's declaration, the city "unleashed the largest, noisiest and most spontaneous celebration in Niagara Falls since Armistice Day in 1918."[217]

Niagarans celebrated immediately, and the din of total celebration lasted until the next day. Church bells, factory and locomotive whistles and automobile horns let the world know that the war was over. Thousands of people braved the rain and converged on the downtown business area. Traffic was at a standstill, and people ventured out of their cars and walked to their destinations. There was singing on the streets. Residents even went so far as to tear up newspapers and magazines and to shower Third Street, in Broadway fashion, with celebratory homemade confetti.

There were also church services that evening. Many people were driven to give thanks, to light votive candles and offer prayers at various places of worship. One woman knelt alone in a front-row seat at Our Lady of Lebanon Church "weeping silently."[218]

It did not end for quite some time. Niagara Falls observed the first day of peace by an almost total cessation of business and industry. It was the first holiday for war workers in over forty-four months. Plants, stores, banks and businesses were closed. The mayor's V-Day committee called for a two-day celebration, and many businesses and plants ceased operations until Friday, August 17.

The city had never seen anything like this in its history and probably never will. One of the most catastrophic wars was finally over, and Niagara Falls was proud of its contributions to victory.

HOMECOMING

Private First Class Nunzio Spacone was thrilled to be on his way home to Niagara Falls, New York. He had served three years in the Pacific with no furloughs. So many times, he had imagined his homecoming. He had made it to the end. So many did not.

It took eleven days by ship from mainland Japan to the West Coast of the United States. He landed in Seattle, Washington, in November

Nunzio Spacone. *Courtesy Nunzio Spacone.*

1945. The residents of Seattle wholeheartedly welcomed him and all the other returning soldiers. But it was here that he learned the terrible news: there was a nationwide railroad strike, and it would put his homecoming on hold. For twenty-one days, he was stuck in Seattle. It was too far to travel from Seattle to Niagara Falls by bus, so he had no choice but to wait for a train.

On Thanksgiving, a family in Seattle opened up their home for him and welcomed Nunzio to celebrate American style. "They treated me like a king," he remembers to this day.[219] Even as he was disappointed he could not be with his family on this first big holiday stateside, it was a memorable occasion because of the kindness of strangers. In fact, Nunzio, who had traveled to so many countries and continents throughout his life, admitted that the very best people are right here in the United States.[220]

Finally, the strike ended, and he boarded the train that would take him as far as Buffalo, New York. From Buffalo, he took a bus to Niagara Falls. It was only 5:00 a.m. when he arrived. He probably could have stayed in Buffalo a little longer so that he could arrive at a decent hour, but he just could not wait any longer. The bus dropped him off at Fifteenth Street and Pine Avenue, and he walked the distance home to Ashland Avenue. He was utterly exhausted from his travels and from carrying all of his belongings by hand. He carried several bags of his gear plus souvenirs, which included two Japanese bayonets and a rifle.

The first thing he did when he arrived at his neighborhood, before going home, was to stop at his neighbor's house. As early as it was, he rapped on the door of the Serchia home. Mrs. Serchia, along with others, had corresponded with Nunzio throughout his time in the war. "Her letters were unlike any of the others," he said.[221] Whereas the others wrote a few lines, Mrs. Serchia wrote four or five pages. Her letters were so interesting, too. In detail, she wrote of the neighborhood and all its people. She kept him in touch with Niagara Falls, and this brought him such great comfort. She was the first person he wanted to see. She opened the door, and she and all of her children rejoiced at Nunzio's homecoming. He was finally home.

THE GI BILL

The Servicemen's Readjustment Act of 1944, also known as the GI Bill, was signed into law on June 22, 1944, by President Franklin Delano Roosevelt. This bill allowed men and women veterans, who, under normal circumstances, would probably not have been able to consider higher education, the opportunity for an education. According to Roosevelt, the bill would allow the servicemen and women to resume their educational or technical training after discharge or to take refresher or retainer courses. This would cover tuition up to $500 per school year and also included the right to a monthly living allowance during the pursuit of studies.[222]

By 1947, 49 percent of all college students in the United States were veterans. By the end of the period of the original GI Bill, on July 25, 1956, 7.8 million World War II veterans had participated in an education or training program.[223] Service in the war had intensified the drive of thousands of veterans to obtain all the levels of education that were possible in order to make themselves more marketable in a strenuous postwar economy.

Over eight hundred veterans had accepted the educational benefits of the GI Bill in the Niagara Falls area by 1946.[224] Most attended Trott Vocational School, programs at Niagara Falls High School, Niagara University and schools in Lockport. Many took apprenticeships or enrolled in on-the-job training.

Dominic Niccola (bottom left) in the GI program at Trott Vocational School. This picture shows the graduates from the School for Junior Tradesmen. *Courtesy Dominic Niccola.*

Dominic Niccola. *Courtesy Dominic Niccola.*

Dominic Niccola, of Niagara Falls, served over two years with the United States Army in India during World War II. Upon returning, he took advantage of the GI Bill's educational programs and attended Trott Vocational School for Junior Tradesmen. He worked for three years at his training and graduated with two diplomas, one from the state and one from the county. Dominic was given $100 toward tools and $100 for books.

The top floor of the Trott Vocational School was reconfigured in the postwar period to be "strictly a G.I. school."[225] The general aim of this program at Trott was to "give the Niagara area war veteran the individual help he needs for a job or to meet college entrance requirements."[226] Pupils ranging in ages from eighteen to thirty attended evening classes at this location. Many of the programs offered at Trott included apprenticeships or on-the-job training. More than four hundred area veterans had taken advantage of Trott's programs by 1946.[227]

For some, Trott acted as a steppingstone to other opportunities. Anthony Eleuteri, a Niagara Falls man who had been captured at the Battle of the Bulge and taken prisoner by the Germans, studied chemistry at Trott in order to help him pass Cornell University's entrance requirements in pre-college work. Duane Jordan, a Pacific war veteran, learned the electrician's trade by taking advantage of the Niagara Falls Federation of Labor's sponsored on-the-job training at Trott. One female veteran of the WAC, Jennie Lucci, also took advantage of Trott's programs and studied English and history.

In 1943, at Niagara University's annual commencement services, Judge Harry S. McDevitt, president of the Philadelphia Court of Common Pleas, spoke of the future. He foresaw the war's end and the need to rebuild a fresh world. Educated men were an integral part of success in the future:

Winning the war is only the first step in the reformation of what we formerly considered a civilized world....Rehabilitating civilization and reestablishing the oppressed peoples of the world on a firm economic basis are problems that only the wisest heads can solve....Civilization must choose between education and catastrophe....The strength, character, reputation and influence of a nation depend upon the education of its citizens.[228]

War Experiences Breed New Ideas

Some returning veterans had learned skills while in the military. Some came up with ideas that would shape their futures, thanks to experiences that they had encountered while in the service.

The aforementioned Nunzio Spacone had just returned from the war in search of a job when his friend Albert "Pee Wee" Proietti came to him with a proposition that would change the history of Niagara Falls.

"Let's make a pizzeria," he told Nunzio. Nunzio laughed out loud. He said that most people would not even be able to say the word "pizzeria." But Pee Wee was insistent. While serving in the European theater, he had been to Naples, Italy, and had seen American GIs line up for blocks to get a slice of "pizza." Nunzio agreed, and he and his partner founded Pee Wee's Pizzeria in 1946 at 721 Nineteenth Street, the very first pizzeria in the city of Niagara Falls.[229]

Some Still Served

For some, the war's end was only the beginning. Private First Class Peter Vendrillo of Niagara Falls had the good fortune to begin basic training as the war in Europe came to a halt and to complete his training as the war with Japan came to a halt. "They knew you were coming," his friends used to laugh.[230] He was supposed to be sent to the Pacific theater of war, but his orders were changed, and he was sent as a part of the occupying forces in Europe.

It was quite an experience for Peter, fresh out of Niagara Falls High School. He wanted to join the U.S. Marine Corps like his cousin "Harp" Hoolihan, but he was too young and his parents wouldn't sign the

Peter Vendrillo while serving with the occupational forces in postwar Europe. *Courtesy Peter Vendrillo.*

permission forms. Instead, he served with the Seventy-First Infantry for one year during the postwar period. For six months, he was in Germany, and for the other six months, he was stationed in Austria.

Perhaps the worst part of Peter's service was the boat ride to Europe, for he was terribly seasick. He had only been on small fishing boats up until then and had no idea that being on a ship would affect him in this manner. His first views of France and Germany were rubble. He was shocked to see with his own eyes the mess the war had left behind. When he finally arrived in Germany, his main task was to guard German POWs. Some of the German POWs were "something to see in person."[231] For the most part, the German people were very friendly to the Americans, he said. That really surprised him, for they had been so terribly crushed during the war.

One of the biggest problems the American GIs faced was billeting. There were no barracks. Instead, they were told to occupy ordinary people's houses. "Some of the houses were absolutely beautiful," Peter said. It bothered him how some of the GIs were disrespectful in these houses and left cigarette butts and a trail of careless, needless destruction.

There were only a few occasions in which Peter felt intimidated by his situation, but mostly it was only his imagination playing tricks on him. At times the sky was kettle black, and he would have to walk from the POW hospital to the place where he was billeting. Some of the prisoners were "pretty hard core," he observed, and he wasn't sure if they would ever pull anything.[232]

One unforgettable experience involved an incident in which he was held responsible for a large group of POWs. He was instructed to take them on a train in the middle of the night to another location, where they would clean up debris. Peter's only help was two Polish officers. He didn't understand Polish, and they didn't understand English, so there was no communication between the men. He was terrified that one of these POWs would get away. How would he even know? However, one of the POWs in a long leather coat, who had probably served as a German officer during the war, took control and spoke to the men for Peter and the Polish officers. "*Achtung mach schnell!*" he snapped, and the men moved in perfect formation. In the end, Peter returned to the camp with all of his men in order. Not one had escaped. Of course, the prisoners really didn't have much to complain about, for they were treated well and fed better than their fellow Germans.

And speaking of the food—Peter had very fond memories of the food in Germany. There were German cooks at the mess hall, and the food was spectacular. He mentioned that he gained a bit of weight because of the sweets. "We ate well over there."[233]

According to Peter, there was nothing the Germans wouldn't do for some C-rations, especially cigarettes and candy bars. At one point, he was billeted in a resort hotel on a lake in Austria. Before the war, royalty would stay at this location. He and his friends enjoyed their time there, especially after they were loaned kayaks for the day by a couple of boys in exchange for some chocolate bars and cigarettes.

Peter had other jobs, too, besides looking after POWs. He was placed in the old library for some time, and he also worked as a clerk. In the office, he worked alongside an Austrian girl named Fritzi. She told him that the Americans should have let the Germans take Russia because Russia was going to be the biggest postwar headache. And her words were not too far from the truth, he remarked.

LEGACY

There is a monument to all American veterans in the city of Niagara Falls at Hyde Park. The stadium at Hyde Park was dedicated on October 17, 1936, with President Franklin Delano Roosevelt and First Lady Eleanor Roosevelt present, along with about forty thousand spectators. Perhaps many veterans of the Second World War find it a fitting place for a memorial to their service as the shadow of their commander in chief looms large in this location's history. The memorial itself was built by the Niagara Falls Veterans Memorial Commission, Inc., and completed in 2013.

Officially, the monument is "dedicated to the 463 warriors who were residents from the city of Niagara Falls who gave their lives in defense of the United States of America."[234] Its main feature is a black granite sarcophagus that contains the personal effects of fallen warriors, including medals, dog

Niagara Falls Veterans Memorial. *Courtesy Tim Baxter.*

World War II Veterans Honor Flight with Senator Maziarz to Washington, D.C. Nunzio Spacone is the fifth veteran from the left in the second row. *Courtesy Nunzio Spacone.*

tags, name tags, photos and letters. The Veterans Wall of Honor is open to any living or deceased veteran who served honorably in the United States military. Their names can be engraved on the wall by completing an application and submitting proof of service.

In July 2015, state senator George Maziarz accompanied a group of veterans from the area on an Honor Flight to visit the World War II Monument and other sites in Washington, D.C. Nunzio Spacone was one of the men who participated in this trip. "It was wonderful," he said. "But I had never seen so many grown men cry."[235]

Serving one's country in a time of war is never easy. Some have answered the call. Regardless if the service required is at home or abroad, it is necessary for victory. And thank goodness so many individuals from Niagara Falls were willing to sacrifice so much during World War II.

NOTES

Introduction

1. Dow, *Anthology*, 25.
2. Ibid., 191.
3. Lincoln, *Collected Works*, 10, 11.
4. Dunlap, "Electrical Kitchen," 54.
5. Dunlap, "Niagara Falls Hydroelectric Power," 537.
6. Feder, "Evolution of an Ethnic Neighborhood," 558.
7. Boston, "Family."
8. Brooks, *Facing the Future*, 15.
9. Ibid., 16.

Chapter 1

10. Letter to the *Niagara Falls Gazette*, written by James W. MacKenzie, n.d. Courtesy Niagara Falls Public Library.
11. Ibid.
12. CBS News, "Almanac: Pearl Harbor."
13. *Niagara Falls Gazette*, "Niagara Falls Is Armed Camp as Troops Man Defense Posts," December 8, 1941.
14. Ibid.
15. Ibid.

16. Ibid., "Falls Soldier Is Reported Killed in Hawaii Action," December 17, 1941.
17. Ibid.
18. Ibid.
19. Ibid., "Mothers Learn Their Sons Are Safe in Hawaii," January 3, 1942.
20. Ibid.
21. Ibid., "Second Navy Man Reported Killed," December 18, 1941.
22. Ibid., "Mothers Learn Their Sons Are Safe."
23. Ibid., "Falls Man Was Pearl Harbor Casualty; Another Shot Down," December 3, 1961.
24. Ibid.
25. Ibid.
26. Ibid., "New Citizens Are Told that the Army Looks to Them," May 17, 1943.
27. Ibid., "Falls Native Shares Father's Personal Written Account of Pearl Harbor Attack," December 6, 2011.
28. Ibid.
29. Ibid.
30. Ibid., "Couldn't Remember Prayers as Bombs Exploded in Hickam Field Attack," December 9, 1943.
31. Ibid.
32. Ibid., "Decorated," May 8, 1942.
33. Ibid., "Falls Man Was Pearl Harbor Casualty."
34. Ibid., "Falls Woman Is Back from Hawaii," January 14, 1942.
35. Ibid., "Falls Mother and Children Home After Undergoing Hawaii Attack," January 6, 1942.
36. Ibid., "Stand in Silent Tribute to Dead in Japanese War," December 9, 1941.
37. Ibid.
38. Ibid., "Bonds Between United States and Canada Tightened by Common War," December 10, 1941.
39. Ibid.
40. Ibid., "No Japanese in City, Police Survey Shows," December 8, 1941.
41. Ibid., "Only Japanese Resident of Falls Sees Attack as Japanese Suicide," December 9, 1941.
42. Ibid.
43. Ibid.
44. Ibid., "Japanese American Proud of Citizenship," March 30, 1958.
45. Ibid
46. Ibid.

47. Ibid., "Start Rounding Up 400 Germans, Italians Classed as Dangerous," December 9, 1941.

48. Ibid., "29 Enemy Aliens Nabbed in Area," December 12, 1941.

49. *Buffalo Courier-Express*, "Contraband Seized in Alien Roundup," March 6, 1942.

50. *Niagara Falls Gazette*, "New Year Message to the People of Niagara Falls," December 31, 1941.

CHAPTER 2

51. Ibid., "Mirrington Is Not Candidate, Letter States," June 1, 1943.

52. Cozzens, "Colonel Peter A. Porter."

53. *Niagara Falls Gazette*, "Private Mirrington Can Take It, Soldier Pals at Fort Niagara Discover," June 13, 1942.

54. Ibid.

55. Ibid.

56. Ibid.

57. Ibid.

58. Ibid.

59. Ibid.

60. Ibid., "Private Mirrington Gets Great Applause," June 15, 1942.

61. Ibid., "Draft Boards at Falls Are Ready to Number Cards," October 24, 1940.

62. Personal letter from Johanna Barthel to Debbie Zucco, July 21, 1995.

63. *Niagara Falls Gazette*, "Women's Army Corps to Celebrate Fourth Anniversary of Founding," May 13, 1946.

64. Ibid., "WACs Safeguard Health of Troops," April 10, 1944.

65. Ibid., "Can You Do Less," May 13, 1944.

66. Ibid., "Mayor Praises Work of WACs," July 27, 1944.

67. Ibid.

68. Ibid., "Falls Girls Join WAC at Ceremony in State Park," November 6, 1943.

69. Ibid.

70. Ibid., "Honor WAC Members," March 13, 1945.

71. *Buffalo News*, "Seventy Years Later, Women's Army Corps Will Be Honored with Medals in Riverside Ceremony," November 2, 2014.

72. *Niagara Falls Gazette*, "To Aid in Local WAVES Recruiting," September 10, 1944.

73. United States Navy, "Facts about SPARS."

CHAPTER 3

74. *Niagara Falls Gazette*, "Believe Cold Weather Hastened 'Armistice' at Army's War Games," August 23, 1940.
75. Ibid., "Some Side Line Chatter from the Army Camps," May 22, 1941.
76. Ibid.
77. Ibid., "Betty Is Lone Girl with 52,000 Troops Engaged in 'Battle,'" August 22, 1939.
78. Ibid., "Some Side Line Chatter."
79. Scime, interview.

CHAPTER 4

80. *Niagara Falls Gazette*, "War Takes Heavy Toll of Niagara Falls Men," August 15, 1945.
81. Ibid., "Joseph Germele Among Niagara's Foremost Heroes of Present War," December 28, 1943.
82. Woodcock, interview.

CHAPTER 5

83. *Niagara Falls Gazette*, "New Warning of Possible Attack Spurs Defense Efforts at Falls," December 10, 1941.
84. Ibid.
85. Source who chooses to remain anonymous, March 2016.
86. *Niagara Falls Gazette*, "Defense Council Appointed for Niagara Falls," February 22, 1941.
87. Ibid., "Fully Trained Auxiliary Police Force to Be Ready in Emergency," November 6, 1941.
88. Ibid., "1,800 Recruits Are Sought for Civilian Defense Work at Falls," November 12, 1941.
89. Ibid., "Niagara Falls Defense Council; Headquarters Divisions," December 10, 1941.
90. Ibid., "New Warning of Possible Attack Spurs Defense Efforts at Falls," December 10, 1941.
91. Ibid., "Drive to Enroll 1,800 Defense Volunteers Is Opened at Falls," November 13, 1941.
92. Ibid., "Seek Volunteers for Air Patrol," December 18, 1941.

93. Ibid., "Plan Training for Inductees," March 23, 1944.

94. Ibid., "Civil Air Patrol Requires Private Fliers, Radio Men," January 22, 1942.

95. Ibid., "Remarkable Record of Wartime Service Made by Red Cross at Falls," 1945 (exact date illegible).

96. Ibid., "Red Cross Asks Blood Donations Here on Friday," November 11, 1941.

97. Ibid., "Remarkable Record."

98. Ibid., "Ambitious Program Is Adopted by Newest Women's Volunteer Group," November 21, 1941.

99. Ibid., "The AWVS, a Splendid Record," June 6, 1944.

100. Ibid., "Old Falls Fence Becomes Scrap Iron to Aid Nation's Struggle," April 21, 1942.

101. Ibid., "Hotel Chef Diligently Salvages All Possible Fats for Use in Explosives," March 16, 1943.

102. Ibid.

103. Ibid., "116 Gazette Carriers Volunteer as Salesmen for Defense Stamps," December 3, 1941.

104. Ibid., "59,142 Defense Savings Stamps Are Sold by *Gazette*'s Carriers," December 27, 1941.

105. Vendrillo, interview.

106. *Niagara Falls Gazette*, "May Postpone Practice Blackout at Falls until after Christmas," December 11, 1941.

107. Ibid., "Seek Approval of State Defense Chief for Blackouts Here December 26," December 18, 1941.

108. Ibid., "Darkness Hides City as Defenses against Attack Tested," December 27, 1941.

109. Ibid.

110. *Union-Sun and Journal*, Lockport, NY, "Falls Illumination Will Be Resumed," October 11, 1944.

111. *Buffalo Courier Express*, "Falls Lighting Reflects Allied Victory Hopes," October 22, 1944.

112. *Niagara Falls Gazette*, "Ask Relief from Gas Conditions," August 10, 1943.

113. Ibid.

114. Ibid.

115. Ibid.

116. Ibid., "War Gas Facts; Is Niagara Falls Really Awake?" February 20, 1943.

117. Borgatti, interview.

118. Ibid.

119. Myers, interview.

120. Myers, *Life Collection of Poetry*.

Chapter 6

121. American Institute of Aeronautics and Astronautics, "Bell Aircraft Plant."

122. Bell Aircraft Corporation, "A Day at Camp Bell," *The Bellringer* 3, no. 7 (June 1943).

123. *Niagara Falls Gazette*, "Niagara Falls to Become Airplane Center," October 29, 1940.

124. Ibid.

125. Ibid.

126. Ibid., "Falls Airport Brought War Plane Plant Here," May 7, 1945.

127. Ibid.

128. Ibid., "Bonhurst Cites New Air Rules," December 11, 1941.

129. Ibid., "Niagara Falls to Become Airplane Center."

130. Norton, *Biography of Lawrence D. Bell*, 72.

131. *Niagara Falls Gazette*, "Bell Aircraft's Tremendous War Job Shown in Annual Statement," May 15, 1945.

132. Ibid., "Story of the Bell Aircraft Plant a Wonderful Record of Enterprise and Achievement," November 1, 1941.

133. Ibid., "Airacobra's Part in Global War Disclosed as Brilliant Chapter in Epic Story of Victory Drive," 1944 (exact date illegible).

134. Ibid., "Airacobra Will Go on Display in Falls Street," September 10, 1943.

135. Ibid., "General George Killed in Crash," April 30, 1942.

136. Wright, "Lieutenant Ivan Baranovsky."

137. Grinberg, *Bringing Her Home*.

138. Wright, "Lieutenant Ivan Baranovsky."

139. Grinberg, *Bringing Her Home*.

140. Matthews, *Cobra!*, 260.

141. *Jamestown New York Post-Journal*, "Famed Test Pilot Will Fly Supersonic Plane," June 13, 1946.

142. Ibid.

143. Ibid.

144. Borgatti, interview.

145. *Niagara Falls Gazette*, "Falls Artist to Exhibit Works," February 13, 1966.

146. Ibid., "Sketches Show Bell War Years," October 13, 1965.

147. *Buffalo Courier Express*, "Soldier-Mechanics Learn to Keep Cobras Ticking," April 18, 1943.

148. Ibid., "Wrecked P-39 Is Reclaimed by Mechanics," October 31, 1943.

149. Ibid.

150. Ibid., "Air Forces to Discontinue Mechanics' School at Bell," October 29, 1944.

CHAPTER 7

151. *Buffalo News*, "Area Planes Fueled War Effort," August 29, 1989.

152. Cowie and Heathcott, *Beyond the Ruins*, 125.

153. Ploughman, *Love Canal*, 7.

154. Ibid.

155. *Niagara Falls Gazette*, "Seek to Remedy Gas Conditions," October 23, 1943.

156. Vanadium Corporation, "Soldiers of Production."

157. Center for Disease Control, "SEC Petition."

158. Ibid.

159. Encyclopedia.com, "Carborundum Company."

160. Gilder Lehrman Institute, "Document #1."

161. Center for Health, Environment and Justice, "Love Canal."

162. Woodcock, interview.

163. Paonessa, interview.

164. Boston, "Blacks in Niagara Falls."

165. Ibid.

166. Ibid.

167. Kimberly-Clark, "Women Enter a Broad Industrial Field," 5.

168. *Life*, "Manpower," 27–30.

169. Ibid.

170. Kimberly-Clark, "How Many Women?" 6–7.

171. *Niagara Falls Gazette*, "Canvass to Reveal Attitude of Women Towards War Plant Jobs," April 15, 1943.

172. Ibid.

173. Ibid., "Niagara Falls Women Trained for Plant Work on Jobs, in Schools," May 15, 1943.

174. Ibid.

175. Ibid., "1,000 Women Workers Are Needed in Niagara Falls Plants at Once," February 23, 1943.

CHAPTER 8

176. Ibid., "Fort Niagara to Be Used by Army in New Program," August 26, 1940.

177. Ingraham, "From Fort Niagara to Guadalcanal," 11–17.

178. *Niagara Falls Gazette*, "Second Group of Draftees Arrives at Fort Niagara," January 22, 1941.

179. Ibid., "Excellent Band Now Established at Fort Niagara," August 19, 1941.

180. Ibid., "New Expanded Library Facilities Opened for Fort Niagara Soldiers," April 19, 1944.

181. Notes from Gretchen Duling, PhD, to author, April 27, 2016.

182. *Niagara Falls Gazette*, "Prisoners Won't Be Coddled Here, M'Dowell Asserts," July 13, 1944.

183. Notes from Duling.

184. Dietz, *Honor Thy Fathers & Mothers*, 167–205.

185. *Niagara Falls Gazette*, "War Prisoner Takes Own Life," August 28, 1945.

186. Ibid., "1,750 Nazis Taken from Fort Niagara," November 29, 1945.

187. Ibid., "Fort Niagara," September 15, 1945.

188. Ibid., "Fort Niagara," September 24, 1945.

CHAPTER 9

189. Ibid., "Start Use of New Ration Books," March 1, 1943.

190. Collingham, *Taste of War*, 112–14.

191. *Niagara Falls Gazette*, "Seek Relief in Meat Emergency," March 22, 1944.

192. Ibid.

193. Hulligan, interview.

194. *Niagara Falls Gazette*, "Victory Gardens Here Now Number More than 1,500," June 3, 1943.

195. Ibid.

196. Ibid., "Victory Garden Group Thankful to City Council," October 19, 1943.

197. Ibid., "Victory Garden Group Seeks to Set New Record," March 29, 1945.

198. Ibid., "Victory Gardens Here Now Number More than 1,500."

199. Ibid., advertisement, June 11, 1943.

200. Kerr Glass Mfg., *Kerr Home Canning Book*, 3.

201. Ibid.

202. *Niagara Falls Gazette*, "Canning Exhibit to Be Held at Church," August 24, 1943.

203. Schloss, *Short Cuts*, front cover.

204. *Lockport Union-Sun and Journal*, "Cookbook Contest Open to Students of County Schools," February 2, 1943.

205. Ibid.

206. *Niagara Falls Gazette*, "Winners in D.A.R. Victory Cookbook Contest Announced," March 16, 1943.

207. Ibid., "Many Economical, Health Building Substitutes for Meat Can Be Made," October 3, 1942.

208. Ibid., "Some Meats Unrationed Under New Plan May Become Palatable Meals," January 31, 1943.

209. Ibid., "Correct Diet for Workers Seen Vital Factor in War Production," October 28, 1942.

210. Ibid.

211. Ibid.

212. Ibid.

213. Ibid.

CHAPTER 10

214. Ibid., "The Golden Key," May 12, 1945.

215. Ibid., "VE Day Is Being Observed Quietly in Niagara Falls," May 8, 1945.

216. Ibid.

217. Ibid., "End of War Brings Wild Celebrations Here," August 15, 1945.

218. Ibid.

219. Spacone, interview.

220. Ibid.

221. Ibid.

222. U.S. Department of Veterans Affairs, "Education and Training."

223. Ibid.

224. *Niagara Falls Gazette*, "Veterans Borrow $2,225,000 from Falls Lending Institutions to Buy, Repair or Remodel Homes," May 31, 1946.

225. Ibid., "Niagara Falls Has Special High School for Veterans," March 24, 1946.

226. Ibid.

227. Ibid.

228. Ibid., "Post War World to Need Educated Men, Niagara University Graduates Are Told," May 17, 1943.

229. Spacone, interview.
230. Vendrillo, interview.
231. Ibid.
232. Ibid.
233. Ibid.
234. Niagara Falls Veterans Memorial, "About the Memorial."
235. Spacone, interview.

BIBLIOGRAPHY

BOOKS

Brooks, David. *Facing the Future: The NFCSD (Niagara Falls City School District) Enters the 21ˢᵗ Century*. Executive summary. Niagara Falls, NY: David Brooks, 2006.

Collingham, Lizzie. *The Taste of War*. New York: Penguin Press, 2012.

Cowie, Jefferson R., and Joseph Heathcott. *Beyond the Ruins: The Meanings of Deindustrialization*. Ithaca, NY: Cornell University, 2003.

Dietz, Suzanne Simon. *Honor Thy Fathers & Mothers: Niagara Frontier's Legacy of Patriotism and Survival*. Youngstown, NY: BeauDesigns, 2008.

Dow, Charles Mason. *Anthology and Bibliography of Niagara Falls*. Vol. I. Albany, NY, 1921.

Duling, Gretchen A. *A Legacy of Trust: The Diary (June 1944–May 1946) and Letters (1944–2005) of Otto Herboth, World War II German Prisoner of War Interned at Fort Niagara, New York*. Youngstown, NY: Old Fort Niagara Association, 2009.

Gold Medal Flour. *War-Time Baking*. N.p., n.d.

Italian Research Group, Lewiston Public Library. *Buon Appetito: Niagara's Early Italian-American Culinary Traditions*. Niagara Falls, NY: Createspace, 2014.

———. *The Italians of Niagara Falls*. Vol. I. Niagara Falls, NY: Createspace, 2015.

———. *The Italians of Niagara Falls*. Vol. II. Niagara Falls, NY: Createspace, 2015.

Kerr Glass Mfg. *Kerr Home Canning Book, National Nutritional Issue, Food for Victory*. N.p., 1942.

Lincoln, Abraham. *Collected Works of Abraham Lincoln*. Vol. II. New Brunswick, NJ: Rutgers University Press, 1953.

Matthews, Birch. *Cobra! Bell Aircraft Corporation, 1934–1946*. Atglen, PA: Schiffer Military/Aviation History, 1996.

Myers, Marie. *A Life Collection of Poetry*. Lockport, NY, 2012.

Neeson, Hugh. *Bell Aircraft/Aerospace Overview: A Brief History of the Past, Larry Bell Era (1956–1996)*. Niagara Falls, NY: Niagara Aerospace Museum, 2003.

Norton, Donald J. *A Biography of Lawrence D. Bell*. Chicago: Nelson-Hall, 1981.

Ploughman, Penelope, PhD, JD. *Love Canal*. Charleston, SC: Arcadia Publishing, 2013.

Schloss, Hannah W. *Short Cuts and Left-Overs*. Cleveland, OH: World Publishing Company, 1942.

Periodicals, Company Newsletters and Pamphlets

Bell Aircraft Corporation. *The Bellringer* 3, no. 7 (June 1943).

———. *The Bellringer* 4, no. 1 (December 1943).

———. *The Bellringer* 4, no. 12 (November 1944).

Boston, Michael B. "Blacks in Niagara Falls, New York: 1865 to 1965, a Survey." *Afro-Americans in New York Life and History*, July 1, 2004.

Bradbury, Bill. "Black Menagerie: Black History Month, a Time to Reflect on How Far We've Come, Need to Go." *Niagara Falls Reporter*, March 4, 2003.

DeCroix, Douglas W. "From Russia…with Log." *Western New York Heritage* 12, no. 3 (Fall 2009): 32–43.

Dunlap, Orrin E. "An Electrical Kitchen." *American Kitchen Magazine* 12, no. 2 (November 1899): 51–55.

———. "The Niagara Falls Hydroelectric Power and Manufacturing Company's New Work." *Electrical Engineer* 20, no. 396 (December 4, 1895): 537–41.

Ingraham, Bob. "From Fort Niagara to Guadalcanal and Back: The World War II Stories of Master Sergeant Ingraham, USAAF." *Fortress Niagara, Newsletter—Journal of the Old Fort Niagara Association* 7, no. 2 (December 2005): 11–17.

Kimberly-Clark. "How Many Women." *Cooperation*, July–August 1943.

———. "Women Enter a Broad Industrial Field." *Cooperation*, May–June 1943.

Life. "Manpower: Sweeping Changes Halt Enlistments, Cut Top Draft Age to 38, Give McNutt Selective Service Control." December 21, 1942, 27.

Percy, John W. "Aviation History on the Niagara Frontier." *Western New York Heritage* 5, no. 3 (Summer 2002): 52–58.

United States Navy. "Facts about SPARS." 1943, 6–7.

Vanadium Corporation of America. "Soldiers of Production: At the Niagara Falls Plant of the Vanadium Corporation." 1942.

Wright, Tim. "Lieutenant Ivan Baranovsky's P-39, an Airacobra's Journey to the Eastern Front…and Back." *Air and Space Magazine*, September 2011.

Interviews

Borgatti, Jean Fortuna. Interview by the author on March 5, 2016.

Hulligan, Peggy-Taylor. Interview by the author on March 16, 2016.

Myers, Marie. Interview by the author on May 4, 2016.

Niccola, Dominic. Interview by the author on March 23, 2016.

O'Connor, John "Jack" Vincent, and Evelyn O'Connor. Interview by the author on October 12, 2014.

Paonessa, Joseph. Interview by the author on March 20, 2016.

Scime, Charleen. Interview by the author on April 29, 2016.

Spacone, Nunzio, and Caroline Spacone. Interview by the author on April 1, 2016.

Vendrillo, Peter. Interview by the author on April 5, 2016.

Woodcock, Harold. Interview by the author on April 22, 2016.

Documentary Films

Barner, Mark. *Production Soldiers: Western New York's Working Women of WWII.* Lewiston, NY: Niagara University, 2003.

Grinberg, Ilya, Hugh M. Neeson and Ira G. Ross Aerospace Museum. *Bringing Her Home: The Story of the Miss Lend-Lease.* Buffalo, NY: Full Circle Studios, 2009.

Articles from the Internet

American Institute of Aeronautics and Astronautics (AIAA). "Bell Aircraft Plant to Be Designated a Historic Aerospace Site." www.aiaa.org/Secondary.aspx?id=14063.

CBS News. "Almanac: Pearl Harbor." December 7, 2014. www.cbsnews.com/news/almanac-pearl-harbor.

Center for Disease Control. "SEC Petition Evaluation Report." www.cdc. gov/niosh/ocas/pdfs/sec/carbco/carbcoer-223-r1.pdf.

Center for Health, Environment and Justice (CHEJ). "Love Canal." chej. org/about-us/story/love-canal.

Cozzens, Frederick Swartwout. "Colonel Peter A. Porter: A Memorial Delivered before the Century, December 1864." archive.org/details/colonelpeterapor02cozz.

Encyclopedia.com. "Carborundum Company." www.encyclopedia.com/doc/1G2-2841900030.html.

Gilder Lehrman Institute of American History. "Document #1: Historical Background and Development of the Love Canal Toxic Chemical Disaster." www.gilderlehrman.org/sites/default/files/inline-pdfs/LoveCanal_DocPack_1_1.pdf.

Niagara Falls Veterans Memorial. "About the Memorial." veteransmemorialniagrafalls.com/index.php.

U.S. Department of Veterans Affairs. "Education and Training." www.benefits.va.gov/gibill/history.asp.

OTHER

Boston, Michael. "Family, the Origin of Everything: Family Case Studies that Represent Dimensions of Black Niagaran History." E-mailed to the author, March 19, 2016.

Feder, H. William. "Evolution of an Ethnic Neighborhood that Became United in Diversity: The East Side, Niagara Falls, New York, 1880–1930." PhD diss., State University of New York at Buffalo, 1999.

INDEX

ABOUT THE AUTHOR

Michelle Ann Kratts has written, edited or contributed to several books of local interest, including *The Missed: Tales of Spirit and Tragic End at Niagara*; *Haunted, True Tales of Niagara*; *Anna Edson Taylor, the Queen of Oakwood*; *Angels on the Battlefield: Niagara's Civil War Past*; *The Italians of Niagara Falls* (Vols. I and II); *Buon Appetito: Niagara's Early Italian American Culinary Traditions*; and *From the Mouth of the Lower Niagara River*. She holds degrees from Niagara University, the University of Toronto and the University of New York at Buffalo. She is presently a librarian at the Lewiston Public Library and lives in Niagara Falls with her husband and three children.

Visit us at
www.historypress.net

....

This title is also available as an e-book